T0302152

The Rise and Decline of the Insurgency in Pakistan's FATA

This book analyzes the emergence, rise, and decline of insurgency by the Pakistani Taliban in Pakistan's North-Western region, also known as Federally Administered Tribal Areas (FATA). It provides a detailed account of the rise and decline of the FATA insurgency and also examines aftereffects of the insurgency.

Offering an in-depth analysis of how insurgency in the FATA began in 2004 after Pakistan entered its military forces into the tribal areas, the author illustrates that the insurgency erupted when state repression on masses is combined with a disruption of the previous *modus vivendi* centered on co-optation of local elites. In the following years, the insurgency became so powerful that most of the FATA region fell under the control of the insurgents. The book further argues that a weak counterinsurgency strategy by the Pakistani government characterised by the over-zealous use of force and a failure to win the support of local communities led the insurgency to become stronger and expand its control. Furthermore, the analysis reveals that a more robust counterinsurgency strategy, relying more on a determined and a judicious use of force and attempts to gain the trust and support of local communities, adopted in the later years led to the collapse of the insurgency. In short, this book offers an explanation of what makes an insurgency more likely to occur and how insurgency escalates and declines. In addition, this book sheds light on recent development in FATA including the merger of FATA with the mainstream Pakistan, the rise of the Pashtun Tahafuz Movement, a non-violent protest movement, and the resurgence of the Pakistani Taliban especially after the Afghan Taliban capture of Kabul in the wake of US withdrawal of forces in Afghanistan.

This book is a timely addition to the literature on South Asian Politics and Security Studies.

Shahzad Akhtar is an Assistant Professor in the School of Integrated Social Sciences and a research fellow at the Centre for Security, Strategy and Policy Research, University of Lahore, Pakistan.

Routledge Studies in South Asian Politics

Pakistan's National Security Approach and Post-Cold War Security
Uneasy Co-existence
Arshad Ali

Political Theory and South Asian Counter-Narratives
Maidul Islam

Islam and Democracy in the Maldives
Zahir Azim

Kashmir in India and Pakistan Policies
Piotr Balcerowicz and Agnieszka Kuszewska

Human Rights Violations in Kashmir
Piotr Balcerowicz and Agnieszka Kuszewska

Law and Conflict Resolution in Kashmir
Piotr Balcerowicz and Agnieszka Kuszewska

Pakistan's Foreign Policy
Contemporary Developments and Dynamics
Ghulam Ali

The Politics of Terrorism and Counter-terrorism in Bangladesh
Saimum Parvez and Mohammad Sajjadur Rahman

The Rise and Decline of the Insurgency in Pakistan's FATA
Shahzad Akhtar

Democratic Governance in Bangladesh
Dilemmas of Governing
Nizam Ahmed

For more information about this series, please visit: www.routledge.com/asianstudies/series/RSSAP.

The Rise and Decline of the Insurgency in Pakistan's FATA

Shahzad Akhtar

LONDON AND NEW YORK

First published 2023
by Routledge
4 Park Square, Milton Park, Abingdon, Oxon OX14 4RN

and by Routledge
605 Third Avenue, New York, NY 10158

Routledge is an imprint of the Taylor & Francis Group, an informa business

© 2023 Shahzad Akhtar

The right of Shahzad Akhtar to be identified as author[/s] of this work has been asserted in accordance with sections 77 and 78 of the Copyright, Designs and Patents Act 1988.

Trademark notice: Product or corporate names may be trademarks or registered trademarks, and are used only for identification and explanation without intent to infringe.

British Library Cataloguing in Publication Data
A catalogue record for this book is available from the British Library

Library of Congress Cataloging-in-Publication Data
A catalog record has been requested for this book

ISBN: 978-1-032-39331-5 (hbk)
ISBN: 978-1-032-39330-8 (pbk)
ISBN: 978-1-003-34925-9 (ebk)

DOI: 10.4324/9781003349259

Typeset in Times New Roman
by Taylor & Francis Books

Dedicated to my wife Maimoona Shaheen, my children Amna, Shaheer and Maryam

Contents

Acknowledgements

Reflecting on my journey of writing this book, it has proved a tough undertaking but worth doing. This humble effort of few years allowed me to produce a piece of writing that finally made its way to get published by an academic publisher and become part of academic scholarship. The feeling of writing a study that affected millions of peoples' lives is appreciating in itself. However, this journey would not have been possible without the kind support of many people including my professors, friends, and family members.

I would like to extend special thanks to Professor Stephen Hoadley, and Professor Chris Wilson at the University of Auckland for their continuous support and encouragement, insightful advice, and critical engagement with my work. Professor Chris Wilson's constructive engagement with my research project deserves special mention, whose crucial guidance enabled me to accomplish this task. Professor Robert G. Patman from the University of Otago provided critical feedback on my earlier draft and aided me to improve the quality of my manuscript. My special gratitude for him for consistently motivating me to publish my research with an international academic publisher.

I am very much grateful to my friends and government officials for assisting me during my field research in Pakistan and providing me the necessary moral and logistic support. I am thankful to the renowned journalist Umar Cheema for providing me access to former Director General ISPR (Inter-services Public Relations) Major General, Asim Bajwa, who in turn organised my visit to the Bajaur Agency (FATA), enabling me to interview several tribesmen and military personnel. I am deeply indebted to Dr Rasheed Ahmad Siddique, Dr Khuram Shahzad, Professor Muhammad Shoaib Pervaiz for trusting my abilities and providing crucial moral courage to pursue high academic standards and excellence in life. My special appreciation for Col. (Retd.), Ansar Jamil who helped me in reaching out to military people who fought against the insurgents in the FATA. I also thank my Pashtun friends, Safdar Dawar, Mr Alamgir Khan Afridi, Shakir Hussain Dawar (District Police Officer) and Zahoor Afridi (Superintendent of Police) for their help and support in approaching tribal leaders of the FATA for interviews. I am also indebted to Dr. Faheem Muhammad who organised my trip to the Tank District in proximity of South Waziristan, enabling me to conduct interviews with several civil and military officials as well as tribesmen hailing from South Waziristan. Without the help of these friends, it would have been almost impossible to get access to the tribesmen of the FATA.

I am deeply obliged to my mother Sakina Bibi and late father Ghulam Qadir whose prayers, guidance and matchless support played a crucial role in setting and achieving my goals in life including my PhD, the highest academic qualification. I extend my appreciation and thanks to my wife and children who waited patiently all the way through the completion of my PhD studies in New Zealand. Her emotional support, encouragement, and assurances of my abilities when I had doubts helped me in a great way to achieve my objectives successfully.

1 Introduction

This book focuses on the dynamics of the Taliban insurgency in the former FATA (Federally Administered Tribal Areas), a region located in Pakistan's North-West along the border with Afghanistan. The seeds of the insurgency surfaced in the FATA in 2004.[1] The Pakistani state has enjoyed only weak control of the FATA since independence in 1947 and there was no insurgency for decades. Following the US invasion and collapse of the Afghan Taliban regime in Afghanistan in late 2001, thousands of the Taliban and Al Qaeda fighters fled in search of safe havens in the FATA where they were greeted warmly by the tribal groups. In addition, local tribes assisted the Afghan Taliban in recruiting tribesmen and madrassa students to fight the US-led international forces in Afghanistan.[2] Most of the militants, who later formed the Tehrik-e-Taliban Pakistan (TTP) in 2007, provided recruits and logistical support to the Afghan Taliban engaged in fighting in Afghanistan.[3] Under pressure from the United States during 2002–2003, Pakistan launched military operations in South Waziristan to capture or kill the foreign militants. The military intervention in the hitherto 'autonomous' tribal areas led to violent confrontations between local militants and the Pakistani troops. As a result, the local militant groups, who were initially focused on fighting in Afghanistan, directed their attention to battling the Pakistani army.[4]

Over a period, these local militant groups united in December 2007 to form the TTP, also known as the Pakistani Taliban. The TTP thereafter served as an umbrella organisation providing local militant groups with a united platform in their aim of fighting the Pakistani state.[5] Joshua T. White noted, "this aggregation function served the TTP leadership in Waziristan by amplifying its voice and reach, but also served the local affiliates by providing them with access to resources."[6] In few years of its establishment in 2007, the TTP developed into a lethal terrorist organization having close links with Al Qaeda, the Afghan Taliban, and other militant groups operating on the Pakistani soil. The TTP perpetrated a number of deadly terrorist attacks in different parts of the country, including an attack on the Pakistani navy's largest airbase in 2011, an attack on Karachi's international airport in 2014, and the most horrific attack at the Army Public School in Peshawar in 2014 that killed approximately150 children.

DOI: 10.4324/9781003349259-1

The Pakistani Taliban maintained a separate organisational structure from the Afghan Taliban. Although the Pakistani Taliban swore allegiance to the Afghan Taliban leader, Mullah Omar, the two groups differed significantly over targets. The Pakistani Taliban carried out attacks against the Pakistani military and security forces inside Pakistan, while the Afghan Taliban focused on fighting against international coalition forces in Afghanistan.[7] Adhering to the Deoband ideology, the TTP declared objectives included fighting US and NATO forces in Afghanistan, implementing sharia law, and waging jihad against the Pakistan Army.[8] Baitullah Mehsud's spokesman, Maulvi Omar, stated in December 2007 that the fundamental aim of the formation the TTP was to consolidate a united front against the Pakistan Army's operations.[9] In mid-2009, the TTP was believed to have between sixteen and twenty thousand members, which was significantly risen to between twenty and twenty-five thousand members in 2012.[10] The fighters were believed to be highly adept at mountain warfare because of their origins in mountainous territory.

The TTP was best described as a decentralized organization with factions across tribal regions with the Mehsud Group forming the core of the TTP. The TTP maintained and nurtured its links with al-Qaeda and other foreign fighters, that provided the organization an international dimension.[11] The TTP's leader Baitullah allowed Al Qaeda to establish its foothold in South Waziristan.[12] In turn, Al Qaeda provided Baitullah with financial and logistical support.[13] In addition, the TTP also established close contacts with Sipahe Sahaba Pakistan (SSP) and Lashkar-e-Jhangvi (LeJ), also known as the Punjabi Taliban which added sectarian dimension to the organization. The TTP was increasingly engaged in sectarian attacks against Shiites.[14] Through the links with other militant groups, the TTP drew significant material and operational benefits. For example, in return for providing safe heavens and training camps to these militant groups in FATA, the TTP gained financial and technical assistance from Al Qaeda and facilitations from the Punjabi militants to conduct attacks in the urban areas of Pakistan.[15]

The TTP adopted suicide bombing as a strategy to put pressure on the government. The TTP established training centres in the FATA region to train new recruits in guerrilla warfare, bomb-making, and suicide attacks.[16] Initially, the main targets of the suicide bombings were security forces and law-enforcement agencies involved in carrying out the operations in tribal areas.[17] Later, the TTP also attempted high-profile terrorist attacks targeting the national level political leadership. The TTP was alleged to have been involved in the assassination of Benazir Bhutto, former female Prime Minister of Pakistan. They were also blamed for carrying out the suicide attacks on Pakistan's former Interior Minister Aftab Sherpao, Asfand Yar Wali and Bashir Bilor of the Awami National Party, and many others. The then Prime Minister Yousuf Raza Gilani escaped a targeted attack by the TTP on September 3, 2008.[18]

The Pakistani Taliban also used terror tactics against the civilian population in the FATA to coerce their submission.[19] The TTP was found involved in the killing of hundreds of pro-government local tribal leaders, with numerous incidents of shooting, kidnapping and beheading.[20] In one attack on 6 November 2008 on an anti-Taliban *jirga* in Salarzai Tehsil, Bajaur Agency, the TTP killed more than 20 tribal leaders including the head of the tribal lashkar, named Malik Fazal Karim Baro.[21] In another incident in November 2008, the Taliban brutally killed 11 local leaders in Chamarkand Tehsil of the Bajaur Agency, beheading them and discarding their dead bodies on the main road.[22] By committing these acts, the TTP sent a clear message to the community that people involved in any activity aimed against the Taliban would meet the same fate.

The TTP's decline started in late 2014 after massive military operations were launched against them. The military's Operation Zarb-e-Azb in 2014 coupled with the US drone campaign hastened the organization decline. The TTP was eventually dislodged from its strongholds in the FATA, which led to the weakening of the organization. By 2016, the TTP disintegrated into several factions and the main leadership fled across the border into Afghanistan. Since then, the TTP militants are largely concentrated in bordering Afghanistan. From their safe havens in Afghanistan, the TTP continued to conduct occasional terrorist attacks on soft targets in Pakistan. In the last couple of years, the current leader of TTP Nur Wali Mehsud has attempted to revive the TTP by bringing back the breakaway factions into the fold of the organization which has potentially increased the overall strength. He also improved discipline in the organization and asked the members to be selective in the violent campaign to reduce the number of civilians casualties. A UN report published in 2020 estimated the number of militants at around six thousand. Emboldened by the Afghan Taliban capture of power in Afghanistan in 2021, the TTP has increased the number of terrorist attacks in Pakistan.

The extent and ferocity of the TTP's insurgency raises several important empirical questions. After decades of quiescence why did the insurgency erupt so suddenly in 2004? Second, what factors facilitated the escalation of the conflict into a powerful insurgency which threatened many areas of Pakistan? And what changed in the Pakistani approach starting from 2009 that led to the gradual decline of the insurgency? Why the Taliban insurgency started, how it became so powerful and what explains its ultimate demise are the subjects of this book. In addition, what has followed in FATA after almost two decades of insurgency and counterinsurgency operations in FATA is also discussed, including integration of FATA into mainstream Pakistan, rise of a social movement known as PTM (Pashtun Tahafaz Movement) and resurgence of the TTP.

The influx of Afghan Taliban and Al Qaeda cannot explain this timing because the region avoided rebellion for a few years after their arrival. This study demonstrates that the timing of the insurgency has more to do with the response of the Pakistani government (although responsibility for the conflict and its atrocities lies with the TTP alone). It is argued that the insurgency started in 2004 when the Pakistani state used repression against the local population and stopped co-optation of the local leaders who were previously given financial and political benefits in return for cooperating with the state. The use of repression against the local people aggravated the pre-existing feeling of grievances, as the FATA endured socio-economic impoverishment because of its long-standing semiautonomous status and minimal state presence that motivated recruitment. However, leadership to the insurgency was provided when the Pakistani state subjected the local leaders to repression while revoking their prestigious status which deprived them of political and economic benefits.

To explain rise and fall of the insurgency, it is argued that the quality of the state's counterinsurgency proved instrumental in terms of whether the rebellion grows or declines over time. The rise of the FATA insurgency was mainly caused by a poor counterinsurgency campaign, characterised by the over-zealous use of force and a failure to win the support of local communities. Conversely, a strong and smarter counterinsurgency relying more on the judicious use of force led to the fall of the FATA insurgency. While the use of a determined and powerful force is certainly important, the targeted nature of this force and attempts to gain the trust and support of local communities were quite important elements in the later counterinsurgency campaign. These very fundamentals marked an effective campaign that finally met with success.

Research Methodology

This section elaborates on the methodology and sources of information used to write this book. This study follows a case study methodology because this methodological approach allows for a close analysis of the various phases of the FATA conflict. The case study approach is a common methodological tool in qualitative research used to generate contingent hypotheses about the causal mechanisms that produce particular outcomes.[23] Hence, the aim of this research is to produce 'thick' within-case analysis of the repression inflicted on local population as well as on the local leaders in the FATA and its presumed cause of the onset of the FATA insurgency.[24]

For the case analysis, process tracing is the primary methodological tool used for qualitative analysis applied in the empirical chapters that follow.[25] Process tracing can be defined as "the analysis of evidence on processes, sequences, and conjunctures of events within a case for the purposes of either developing or testing hypotheses about causal mechanisms that might causally explain the case."[26] Among the different varieties of process-tracing such as 'detailed narrative', 'general explanation', and the 'use of hypothesis and generalisation', this study will use 'analytical explanation'. The analytical explanation form of the process-tracing approach "transforms a historical narrative into an analytical causal explanation couched in the explicit theoretical forms."[27] In addition, the process tracing method "attempts to identify the intervening causal process – the causal chain and causal mechanism – between an independent variable (or variables) and the outcome of the dependent variable."[28] Therefore, the use of process tracing requires a detailed within-case analysis of linking events to explain the causal mechanism under examination. To do the analysis, different sources commonly used in qualitative studies, such as "histories, archival documents, [and] interview transcripts" have been used.[29]

This study is also comparative that included inter-temporal comparison to deepen analysis of the rise and decline of the FATA insurgency. The comparative method is used to establish the empirical relationship among two or more variables.[30] The comparative method consists of "comparing instances in which [a] phenomenon does occur, with instances in other respects similar in which it does not."[31] Therefore, a comparison of two time periods, characterised by poor and strong counterinsurgency policies executed by Pakistan, is carried out. This temporal comparison helps to understand when and why the FATA insurgency became so powerful and when and why it ended.

Regarding the sources of data collection, this book uses both primary and secondary sources of information. To gather primary data, in-depth semi-structured interviews were conducted in different parts of Pakistan including Islamabad, Peshawar, Tank district and Bajaur Agency. The selection of the interview participants included military officials who served in FATA as well as government officials and the people belonging to the FATA including tribal leaders, especially from the South Waziristan, North Waziristan and Bajaur agencies. To diversify sources of information, independent observers like scholars, researchers and journalists were interviewed. My sample of participants was designed to gain as much information from as broad a spectrum of views as possible.[32] The range of interviews was quite flexible because the number of interviews depended on the variety of information coming from different participants. After conducting sixty interviews, it became evident that further interviews would be redundant because the informants began to repeat information already obtained. Furthermore, the information is gleaned by accessing newspaper archives. Journal articles, books and reports of national and international think tanks were consulted to gain secondary information. The case study qualitative approach used in this book allowed the use of information from varied sources to produce an in-depth analysis of a complex social inquiry.[33]

Structure of the Book

The first chapter accounts for the onset of the FATA insurgency. Repression by the state is generally considered very crucial in stimulating an insurgency because it generates anger which helps insurgents with recruitment. However, in some cases repression does not induce insurgency, rather, it suppresses insurgency before it begins. The FATA case brings nuances to the role of repression in triggering insurgency. How repression worked in the case of FATA insurgency, this chapter argues that the state used repression against people which incited recruitment and at the same time inflicted repression on local leaders by ending their long-held co-optation which provided leadership to the insurgent movement. This is how the FATA insurgency took off. Due to the increasing pressure from the United States in 2004, the Pakistani military carried out several military operations with indiscriminate use of force which in turn aggravated the grievances of the local population. Simultaneously, the state overturned decades-old co-optation of local leaders by depriving them of their political and economic opportunities. The use of repression provided recruits for insurgency and putting an end to co-optation of local leaders provided leadership, thus allowing the insurgency to occur.

The second chapter explains the escalation the FATA insurgency by arguing that the Pakistani government initially exercised weak counter-insurgency policies in the FATA which permitted the insurgency to survive and grow stronger. A reluctant participant in the US-led War on Terror, the Pakistani government lacked the necessary political will to take the threat of insurgency seriously. The lack of political will led to the half-hearted and under-resourced military operations which were largely unsuccessful in con-trolling the insurgency. Inappropriate approaches and lack of counter-insurgency training accompanied by using indiscriminate force caused civilian deaths, injury and damage which alienated local tribesmen and helped the insurgents to gain recruits from the local population. Insufficient and incompetent local security forces left the local population at the mercy of the insurgents' coercive tactics. Finally, the Pakistani state conducted negotiations with the insurgents when they were becoming powerful. Thus, a weak counterinsurgency by the Pakistani government was largely responsible for empowering the insurgency.

The third chapter argues that a subsequent stronger counterinsurgency effort by the Pakistani government led to the weakening the FATA insurgency. After the TTP had made significant gains in the FATA and threatened government control in other parts of the country, the Pakistani government began to take the threat more seriously and the political will to defeat the insurgency grew accordingly. Following this, the conventional forces were trained and reconfigured into counterinsurgency forces and provided with the neces-sary counterinsurgency weapons and equipment. Capable troops were employed in sufficient numbers and necessary force was used to destroy the insurgents' infrastructure. After destroying the militants' military capability and dismantling their control over the territory and the population, the Pakistani military forces were stationed there to deny any space to insurgents to continue their activities. In addition, a more discriminate use of force was prescribed to avoid collateral damage. These counterinsurgency mea-sures forced the TTP leaders and their foot soldiers to flee across the border in Afghanistan thus ending their hold in the FATA region. The government of Pakistan has also made some efforts for bringing socioeconomic development in the region, however, these measures have so far proved to be too little and ineffective.

The fourth chapter discusses how the FATA has evolved after almost two decades of insurgency and counterinsurgency operations. In recent years, the FATA region has witnessed significant changes such as abolishing of its semi-autonomous status and bringing into more formal control of the state, the rise of PTM, and resurgence of the TTP. The FATA has been merged with the neighbouring province Khyber Pakhtunkhwa (KPK) through a constitutional amendment. However, the process of integration has proved far too slow which spawned resentment. The continued presence of military forces in the region has further aggravated those negative feelings. This led to the rise of PTM, a nonviolent social movement, which demands constitutional rights for the people of FATA and has attracted support of the wider Pashtun population. The PTM demands included permanent end to the military troops in the region, provision of basic rights to the people of FATA and improvement of socio-economic conditions. Taking advantage of these tensions, the TTP has attempted to resurrect itself in the region which poses serious challenges to the newly established writ of the Pakistani government. Several splinter groups have reunited with the TTP over the last couple of years which has potentially increased its strength and outreach, reflected in the increasing number of attacks on the security forces. The return of the Afghan Taliban to power in Kabul in 2021 after the American forces relinquished their control of the country has provided immense boost to the TTP. The Afghan Taliban freed hundreds of TTP militants from Afghan jails who celebrated the Taliban victory and vowed to carry out fight against the Pakistani state. Without adequately addressing the grievances of the FATA population, durable peace in the region would remain elusive.

Notes

1 Brian Cloughley, "Insurrection in Pakistan's Tribal Areas," *Pakistan Security Research Unit, Brief No 29* (2008), 1–8.
2 Mona Kanwal Sheikh, *Guardians of God: Inside the Religious Mind of the Pakistani Taliban* (New Delhi: Oxford University Press, 2016).
3 Hassan Abbas, "A Profile of Tehrik-i-Taliban," *CTC Sentinel* 1, no. 2 (2008).
4 Qandeel Siddique, *Tehrik-E-Taliban Pakistan: An Attempt to Deconstruct the Umbrella Organization and the Reasons for Its Growth in Pakistan's North-West* (Copenhagen: DIIS Reports/Danish Institute for International Studies, 2010), 10.
5 Samir Puri, *Pakistan's War on Terrorism: Strategies for Combating Jihadist Armed Groups Since 9/11* (New York: Routledge, 2012), 75.
6 Joshua T. White, *Islamic Politics and US Politics in Pakistan's North-West Frontier* (Arlington: Centre on Faith & International Affairs at the Institute for Global Engagement, 2008), 65.
7 Syed Saleem Shahzad, "Taliban Wield the Ax Ahead of New Battle," *Asia Times Online*, January 24, 2008.
8 Hassan Abbas, "A Profile of Tehrik-i-Taliban," *CTC Sentinel* 1, no. 2 (2008).

 9 Paul Staniland, Asfandyar Mir, and Sameer Lalwani, "Politics and Threat Perception: Explaining Pakistani Military Strategy on the North West Frontier," *Security Studies* 27, no. 4 (2018): 535–74.
10 Amira Jadoon, *The Evolution and Potential Resurgence of the Tehrik-i-Taliban Pakistan* (Washington DC: United States Institute of Peace, 2021), 11.
11 Arabinda Acharya, Syed Adnan Ali Shah Bukhari, and Sadia Sulaiman, "Making Money in the Mayhem: Funding Taliban Insurrection in the Tribal Areas of Pakistan," *Studies in Conflict & Terrorism* (2009): 97.
12 "Spotlight Falls on Taliban Man Accused of Murdering Benazir," *Daily Times*, January 28, 2008.
13 "Spotlight Falls on Taliban Man."
14 Sheikh, *Guardians of God*, 38.
15 Abbas, "Defining the Punjabi Taliban."
16 Iqbal Khattak, "Six Key Militants Outfits Operating in Data," *Daily Times*, January 29, 2008.
17 Abbas, "Defining the Punjabi Taliban," 70.
18 "TTP Claims Responsibility," *Daily Times*, September 4, 2008.
19 Rohan Gunaratna and Khuram Iqbal, *Pakistan: Terrorism Ground Zero* (London: Reaktion Book, 2011), 70.
20 Gunaratna and Iqbal, *Pakistan: Terrorism Ground Zero*, 71.
21 Gunaratna and Iqbal, *Pakistan: Terrorism Ground Zero*, 71.
22 Akhtar Shehzad, "TTP Claims Responsibility, Tells Govt to Stay Away," *The News*, June 26, 2008.
23 Jack S. Levy, "Case Studies: Types, Designs, and Logics of Inference," *Conflict Management and Peace Science* 25, no. 1 (2008): 5–8.
24 Andrew Bennett and Colin Elman, "Qualitative Research: Recent Developments in Case Study Methods," *Annual Review of Political Science* 9 (2006): 468–72.
25 For details on theoretical and methodological factors to consider when applying the process tracing method, see, David Collier, "Understanding Process Tracing," *Political Science and Politics* 44, no. 4 (2011): 823–30.
26 Andrew Bennett and Jeffrey T Checkel, "Process Tracing: From Philosophical Roots to Best Practices," in *Process Tracing: From Metaphor to Analytic Tool* (Cambridge: Cambridge University Press, 2013).
27 Alexander L. George and Andrew Bennett, *Case Studies and Theory Development in the Social Sciences* (Cambridge, MA: MIT Press, 2005), 211.
28 George and Bennett, *Case Studies and Theory Development*, 206.
29 George and Bennett, *Case Studies and Theory Development*, 206.
30 Arend Lijphart, "Comparative Politics and the Comparative Method," *The American Political Science Review* 65, no. 3 (1971): 683.
31 Lijphart, "Comparative Politics and the Comparative Method," 687.
32 Sharan B. Merriam, *Qualitative Research in Practice: Examples for Discussion and Analysis* (San Francisco: Jossey-Bass, 2002).
33 Merriam, *Qualitative Research in Practice.*

Bibliography

Abbas, Hassan. "A Profile of Tehrik-i-Taliban." *CTC Sentinel* 1, no. 2 (2008): 1–3.
Abbas, Hassan. "Defining the Punjabi Taliban Network." *CTC Sentinel* 2, no. 4 (April2009): 1–3.
Acharya, Arabinda, Syed Adnan Ali Shah Bukhari, and Sadia Sulaiman. "Making Money in the Mayhem: Funding Taliban Insurrection in the Tribal Areas of Pakistan." *Studies in Conflict & Terrorism* (2009): 95–108.

Bennett, Andrew, and Colin Elman. "Qualitative Research: Recent Developments in Case Study Methods." *Annual Review of Political Science* 9 (2006): 455–476.

Bennett, Andrew, and Jeffrey T Checkel. "Process Tracing: From Philosophical Roots to Best Practices." In *Process Tracing: From Metaphor to Analytic Tool.* Cambridge: Cambridge University Press, 2013.

Cloughley, Brian. "Insurrection in Pakistan's Tribal Areas." Pakistan Security Research Unit, Brief no. 29, 2008.

Collier, David. "Understanding Process Tracing." *Political Science and Politics* 44, no. 4 (2011): 823–830.

George, Alexander L. and Andrew Bennett. *Case Studies and Theory Development in the Social Sciences.* Cambridge, MA: MIT Press, 2005.

Gunaratna, Rohan. and Khuram Iqbal. *Pakistan: Terrorism Ground Zero.* London: Reaktion Book, 2011.

Jadoon, Amira. *The Evolution and Potential Resurgence of the Tehrik-i-Taliban Pakistan.* Washington DC: United States Institute of Peace, 2021.

Kanwal Sheikh, Mona. *Guardians of God: Inside the Religious Mind of the Pakistani Taliban.* New Delhi: Oxford University Press, 2016.

Khattak, Iqbal. "Six Key Militants Outfits Operating in Data." *Daily Times,* January 29, 2008.

Levy, Jack S. "Case Studies: Types, Designs, and Logics of Inference." *Conflict Management and Peace Science* 25, no. 1 (2008) 1–18.

Lijphart, Arend. "Comparative Politics and the Comparative Method." *The American Political Science Review* 65, no. 3 (1971): 682–693.

Merriam, Sharan B. *Qualitative Research in Practice: Examples for Discussion and Analysis.* San Francisco, CA: Jossey-Bass, 2002.

Puri, Samir. *Pakistan's War on Terrorism: Strategies for Combating Jihadist Armed Groups Since 9/11.* New York: Routledge, 2012.

Shehzad, Akhtar. "TTP Claims Responsibility, Tells Govt to Stay Away." *The News,* June 26, 2008.

Shahzad, Syed Saleem. "Taliban Wield the Ax Ahead of New Battle." *Asia Times Online,* January 24, 2008.

Siddique, Qandeel. *Tehrik-E-Taliban Pakistan: An Attempt to Deconstruct the Umbrella Organization and the Reasons for Its Growth in Pakistan's North-West.* Copenhagen: DIIS Reports/Danish Institute for International Studies, 2010.

"Spotlight Falls on Taliban Man Accused of Murdering Benazir." *Daily Times,* January 28, 2008.

Staniland, Paul, Asfandyar Mir, and Sameer Lalwani. "Politics and Threat Perception: Explaining Pakistani Military Strategy on the Northwest Frontier." *Security Studies* 27, no. 4 (2018): 535–574.

"TTP Claims Responsibility." *Daily Times,* September 4, 2008.

White, Joshua T. *Islamic Politics and US Politics in Pakistan's North-West Frontier.* Arlington: Centre on Faith & International Affairs at the Institute for Global Engagement, 2008.

2 Repression, Co-optation and Insurgency in the FATA

Many scholars of insurgency claim that state repression tends to trigger an insurgency.[1] State violence dramatically increases the already existing feelings of economic and political marginalization. It also provides incentives to avoid the collective action problem and facilitates recruitment process.[2] However, it is not necessary that repression always leads to an armed rebellion. Most importantly, repression under certain condition does not provide sufficient condition to induce insurgency. When the state shares powers with local elites while providing economic and other opportunities, then these elites do not find inspiration in posing opposition even when state violence generates extensive public frustration. However, insurgency is likely to take off when there is a collapse of this *modus vivendi* between state and local elites, to enhance state control of the region. In FATA, the Pakistani state previously co-opted local elites by providing them with economic and political incentives which largely avoided insurgency for many decades before 2004. In 2004, the State violence and repression coupled with ending of co-optation of local leaders played an instrumental role in the eruption of rebellions in Pakistan's FATA.[3]

This chapter argues that under pressure from the US in 2004 the Pakistani military used heavy force against the local tribes which aggravated the pre-existing feelings of economic and pollical grievances. This generated public frustrations at the grassroots level. However, this does not provide sufficient conditions for the onset of insurgency, which means repression alone lacks the power to explain the phenomenon. It was the Pakistani state's dramatic change in its approach towards the local elites of the region who along with marginalization faced repression during 2004 that provided the necessary leadership for the insurgency to erupt. In other words, while repression was crucial in stimulating the insurgency, also important was the state's sudden ending of a long tradition of patronage to local elites.

The FATA before 2004

Since Pakistan took over after the end of the British rule in 1947, the FATA tribes largely remained quiescent and did not pose any serious opposition to

DOI: 10.4324/9781003349259-2

the state.[4] After getting independence in 1947, the Pakistani state did not change the status of the region and followed the British style of administration.[5] After the British failed to subdue the tribes, they developed an indirect method of administration in the area where local leaders helped the former to keep the tribes in check in return for subsidies and allowances for them.[6] The British government introduced a specific set of laws known as the Frontier Crimes Regulations (FCR) to oversee tribal matters. These laws were derived from the centuries old Pashtun customs and traditions.[7] The Pakistani state inherited this approach from the British colonial masters.

Under Pakistan's administration, the FATA region remained short of full integration into the country because of its remote rugged and mountainous terrain and the tribes' disdain for any state control. Unlike the British, the Pakistani state afforded more autonomy to the region while withdrawing military personnel and dismantling military cantonment from the tribal territory.[8] To appease the tribes, the first governor general of Pakistan, Muhammad Ali Jinnah, told a tribal jirga (assembly of tribal elders) at Peshawar in April 1948 that: "Pakistan has no desire to unduly interfere with your internal freedom ... so long as you remain loyal and faithful to Pakistan."[9] In the same speech Jinnah endorsed the continuation of the allowances they received during the British rule, and said:

> You have also expressed your desire that the benefits, such as your allowances and khassadari, that you have had in the past and are receiving, should continue. Neither my government nor I have any desire to modify the existing arrangements except in consultation with you.[10]

In the following decades, the Pakistani state persisted with this approach of providing stipends and payments to the local leaders which helped keeping the tribes calm and peaceful. The government agent also known as (Political Agent) distributed money to the local leaders for development purposes such as health and education, but most of this funding was corrupted.[11] However, in return, the tribes remained friendly and supportive to the Pakistani state policies.[12] Because of limited state presence and control, the region suffered enormously in terms of socioeconomic and political development. Most the FATA population lives below the poverty line. Politically, the region also remained underdeveloped as the adult franchise was only extended in 1997.[13] Although FATA got representation in the Pakistani parliament, but the Article 247(b) of the country's Constitution stripped them of any power to take part in the legislative affairs of the region.[14]

Despite the poor development indicators, the region did not see any insurgency, primarily because of the state co-optation of local leaders.[15] Most importantly, hitherto, the government policy of respecting traditional authority and co-opting local leaders with largesse including political and economic opportunities, disincentivized rebellion from the FATA tribes.[16]

However, the 2004 insurgency marks the end of tribes' peaceful relationship with the Pakistani state.

Post-September 11 FATA

Following the US invasion of Afghanistan in the wake of the 9/11 terror attacks, this *modus vivendi* was shaken. Following their defeat in October 2001, thousands of the Afghan Taliban and Al Qaeda members fled across the border, looking for safe havens in FATA. The tribal groups of FATA welcomed these foreign militants due to ethnic and Islamic ties. They also supported the Afghan Taliban in launching attacks across the border in Afghanistan by providing logistical support and facilitating recruitment. Therefore, from 2002 the US pressured the Pakistani state to capture or kill the foreign fighters hiding in the tribal areas to stop attacks inside Afghanistan.

The government withstood US pressure in attacking the tribes and sought tribal leaders' cooperation in driving the foreign militant out of the region. This approach was consistent with the way the Pakistani governments had handled the tribes previously which enabled the state to avoid disrupting traditional power structures or its longstanding arrangement with local leaders.[17] Although security forces carried out a number of search operations which created some tensions, but the government overall approach did not stripped the local leaders of their traditional powers and they continued to receive allowance and other benefits from the state.[18] Therefore, there was some periodic violence but organized and consistent violence was largely absent. Even, the influx of foreign militants in the region does not provide explanation for occurrence of insurgency. Insurgency erupted in 2004 only when the state adopted indiscriminate violence against the local people and marginalized the local leaders by stripping them of their powers which they traditionally shared with the government.

Insurgency in FATA in 2004: Repression and Ending of Co-optation of Local Leaders

This section demonstrates how repression against the local tribal population aggravated preexisting feelings of marginalization, thus creating environment for the opposition of the state. Most importantly, the ending of co-optation of the local leaders provided crucial leadership necessary to trigger insurgency in 2004. The following section demonstrates how repression galvanized recruitment for the insurgency.

Repression and Insurgency

A significant amount of theoretical literature focuses on the role of largely static phenomena or structural conditions such as inequalities and other grievances,[19] state strength,[20] demography or natural phenomena,[21] in explaining insurgency. These accounts fall short of explaining why a rebellion emerged at one point in time and not before. Although grievances arising from economic or political marginalization provide necessary conditions for a rebellion, they are not sufficient to mark the onset of an insurgency, nor do they predict the timing of the onset of insurgency.

Recognizing the importance of grievances and other structural conditions, a few scholars have been paying attention on the use of state repression in explaining onset of insurgency. Academics have primarily focused on the use of state repression during the earliest stages of rebellion. Repression usually generates public anger, portrays government as brutal, which motivate people to join a rebel movement.[22] For example, Elisabeth Wood, in her investigation of the Salvadoran civil war, observed that use of repression aggravated peasants' perception of the government as deeply unjust, pushing many to join the rebels' movement.[23] State violence therefore affects the collective action problem enabling a nascent rebel movement to get recruits.[24] As Jeff Goodwin asserts while giving repression precedence over economic or political grievances: "Revolutionary movements are not simply or exclusively a response to economic exploitation or inequality, but also and more directly a response to political oppression and violence."[25]

Yet repression can yield different outcomes in different contexts. State violence sometimes crushes a movement even before it takes off; but in some other cases, it leads to a dramatic increase in resistance.[26] Most studies which explain these different outcomes focused on the form and targets of the repression, while scholars have attempted to explain these varied outcomes.[27] In particular, forms of repression whether targeted or indiscriminate and targets of repression, whether civilians or non-civilians, plays a crucial role in determining whether an insurgency begins or not.[28] If the state adopts indiscriminate violence or targets the civilians or noncombatants, people not only feel resentment, but their sense of insecurity also heightens. This is how state violence stimulates grassroots anger and facilitates recruitment into rebel organizations.[29]

The Pakistani state's use of repression had resulted into a similar outcome. Pakistani state's indiscriminate violence against the local population generated anti-state feelings which in turn mobilized opposition against the state. In the beginning of 2004, the Pakistani government faced intensive US pressure to launch aggressive military operation in the FATA. Ignoring Pakistan's deployment of around 70,000 Pakistani regular troops along the border and the arrest of several important Al Qaeda members from different parts of Pakistan,[30] the US officials alleged that Al Qaeda militants and their local supporters continued to launch attacks in Afghanistan from their sanctuaries in Pakistan's tribal areas.[31] In one such attack, more than 300 people were killed, including US and Afghan soldiers.[32] Therefore, Gen. David Barnes, the Commander of the US forces in Afghanistan, asked the Pakistani government to carry out tough military operations in FATA.[33] In a visit to Pakistan, CIA Director George Tenet also demanded serious operations to capture Al Qaeda fighters.[34] To motivate Pakistan further, the United States promised a generous aid package of US\$3 billion and designated Pakistan the status of non-NATO ally in return for intensive military operations in the tribal areas.[35]

The Pakistani government in 2004 bowed to US pressure and launched intensive military operations in different parts of the FATA.[36] On 16 March 2004, the military carried out an operation involving14,000 military and paramilitary troops in Kaloshah village, South Waziristan agency.[37] Similarly, in 2005, the military launched another operations against Mehsud tribes in South Waziristan.[38] These military operations amounted to the violation of tribal norms and custom and disregard of the traditional autonomy, the region enjoyed for long periods of time.[39] It is important to highlight that the Frontier Corps, a paramilitary force mostly drawn from Pashtun population, had previously undertaken search operations in the tribal areas. However, more recently, military personnel unaccustomed to tribal traditions and norms had become increasingly involved in operations against the tribes.[40] Most importantly, local tribal leaders were sidelined while launching these military operations.[41] This disregard for the tribal leaders and violation of tribal norms and customs generated animosity and anti-military feelings among the tribes.[42] A former political agent who served in FATA contended that the use of troops was most likely to engender opposition among the local tribes.[43]

The military used massive power against the tribal population. In a military operation carried out in March 2004 in South Waziristan, "largest and biggest in any of the federally-administered tribal regions since Pakistan's creation,"[44] a total force of around 14,000 troops was used, involving the use of helicopter gunships.[45] An indiscriminate use of power caused massive human rights abuses involving civilian casualties.[46] For example, in a military operation in the Shakai Valley of South Waziristan in June 2004, the military bombed tribal communities with Precision Guided Missiles (PGMs) resulting in significant causalities.[47] In addition, the helicopter gunships targeted a van carrying civilians who were moving to a safer location.[48] In another instance, 17 people including women and children were killed during a military operation in the Waziri Kot area located on the outskirts of Miramshah, North Waziristan, in July 2005.[49] In addition, the houses of local tribesmen were also destroyed during the military operation.[50] A local journalist contended that the overwhelming use of force during operations caused "more deaths and destruction,"[51] which generated bitter feelings among the tribesmen.[52] These atrocities led the tribesmen to allege that "Rulers [Pakistani government] were engaged in the genocide of innocent tribesmen just to please the United States."[53]

In another agency of FATA named Bajaur, the military operations targeted a religious school also called *madrassa* which led to the civilian causalities and serious human rights violations. A local journalist described the severity of the attack in Bajaur: "The bodies were burnt. Pieces of flesh were strewn all over the place. Rescuers were picking up body parts and putting them in bags."[54] Human Rights Watch (HRW) noted that "The scale of the deaths point to use of excessive force in the extreme, with no or little effort to minimize loss of life."[55] Various local accounts confirmed an Amnesty International report that recorded human rights abuses committed during the military operations. The report highlighted that despite the hoisting of white flags on their houses to differentiate them as non-combatants, the civilian population was often targeted by the security forces.[56] Indiscriminate killings by the military forces transformed the once neutral population into enemies of the state. According to journalist Rahimullah, "Missile attacks and bombings invariably cause collateral damage and contribute to the intensity of hatred against the [Pakistani government] attackers."[57]

The government repression took an ugly shape with the imposition of economic sanctions which affected the livelihood of common people. Such economic blockades by the government immensely added to the frustrations of the local tribes. The economic blockade was termed a violation of basic human rights.[58] A blockade in the Wana area of South Waziristan prevented 80 percent of farmers transporting fruit and vegetables to the market, depriving them of their main source of livelihood.[59] Describing the frustrations of the local people, an eminent journalist, Rahimullah Yusufzai, maintained, "Military operations and punitive measures such as economic sanctions ... alienated most of the people."[60] Most of the shops in the main market of Miranshah bazar were destroyed due to artillery fire. Moreover, the main hospital, schools, and college were severely damaged during the operation and several main roads were closed for an indefinite time.[61] An English daily contended in its editorial, "closures of markets, and local economic blockades for months ... caused thousands of innocent tribesmen unmerited suffering, alienating the local population."[62]

Massive human right abuses and civilian losses because of the indiscriminate use of force turned the local people against the state and its security forces. This pushed the common tribesmen to join the forces who were gearing up to oppose the state.[63] According to Hasan Abbas, the indiscriminate targeting of civilians pushed them to support those who were engaged in fighting the government security forces.[64] According to another analyst, Beena Butool, the Pakistan military's indiscriminate and heavy use of force generated anti-military and anti-state feelings which significantly contributed the 'peoples' revolt' against the state.[65]

Ending of Co-optation of Local Leaders and Insurgency

While this repression was necessary for the onset of insurgency, however, it was not sufficient alone. Also necessary was a dramatic change in the government's approach towards the local elites that used force against then while ending their longstanding co-optation. This created a leadership vacuum which was filled by the more militant elements in the tribal society. I contend that repression is more likely to cause rebellion when the state dismantles a past arrangement of patronage and co-optation with local elites. When state repression on masses is coupled with a disruption of the previous *modus vivendi* centered on co-optation of local elites, insurgency becomes more likely. The indiscriminate use of force amounts to human rights abuses and generates local anger which tends to aggravate the feelings of being marginalized in the context of deep-rooted poor governance. Most importantly, dismantling of this longstanding arrangement between the state and local leaders facilitates ways to create the leadership necessary for a rebel movement to take off. Previously co-opted elites are either radicalized and become leaders of the rebel movement or are marginalized in favor of more militant leaders.

Some theoretical insights on leadership informs vividly how important leadership is for the success of any social movement. Leadership is quite crucial to most forms of social movement because "Leaders are critical to social movements: they inspire commitment, mobilize resources, create and recognize opportunities, devise strategies, frame demands, and influence outcomes."[66] As Vasabjit Bannerjee has pointed out, rebellions require the collaboration of both elite classes and peasants.[67] Some other studies highlight how state patronage and co-optation is crucial in avoiding conflict.[68] In his research on revolutions, Goldstone argued local elites who serve as intermediary between people and the regime play an important role in the stability and a lack of challenge to the state.[69] Margaret Levi wrote that in order to "tame the violence within the country's borders, it is necessary to offer powerful constituents enough in the way of benefits to retain their loyalty."[70] In addition, some scholars have argued that people are more likely to rebel when they lose previously held autonomy. Ted Gurr found that "rebellion (in the 1980s) was mainly a response to the group's historical loss of autonomy and differential political status."[71] David Siroky and John Cuffe note that groups who are deprived from the previously enjoyed autonomy are more likely to engage in separatist insurgency.[72] Those groups which have recently lost autonomy often have both the incentive (grievance) and the leadership and capacity (through recent self-government and revenue collection) to pursue secession.

Pakistani state increasing repression in 2004 also targeted the local leaders by ending of co-optation which stripped them of the traditional power. Ending of co-optation of local leaders also included stoppage of their allowances, financial benefits, and other privileges. This marginalization of local leaders created leadership void which was filled with radical individuals. The first step in the marginalization of the local leaders occurred when military became increasingly involved in the FATA affairs while sidelining the Political Agent. The Pakistani Army presence and military actions in FATA in 2004, discredited the role of the Political Agent that had long maintained relationships with tribal society and leaders. This development was quite important given the fact that the Pakistani government abolished permanent military presence in the FATA since 1948. The Pakistani army seriously lacked knowledge of local customs and experience of dealing with the local leaders and the tribal society. In contrast, the PA and its supporting staff held deep knowledge of the tribal customs and norms and knew the art of keeping check on tribes through the local leaders. A former Interior Secretary who served as a political agent in the tribal areas stated: "the political agent has been replaced by the Army. Captains, majors and colonels are dealing directly with the tribes, who don't know the ABCs of the tribal area. They don't know how to deal with them, with the result that it is a mess."[73] Beena observed that the involvement of "the Pakistani army discredited the tribal process", arguing further, "The tribesmen were accustomed to dealing with the PA [Political Agent] ... saw the army's intervention as a violation of FCR."[74] Rahimullah affirmed this view that with the army into the driving seat, the political administration led by Political Agent and assisted by local leaders rendered almost irrelevant.[75]

The tribal leaders further felt marginalized when the military carried out operations without their consultation. Military operations were undertaken in haste primarily under pressure from the United States. A former political agent in the FATA, Khalid Aziz, noted that "The traditional way of dealing with the tribes was hastily abandoned," and use of massive military power "rendered the local administration and their protégés the tribal elders, ineffective."[76] Beena observed, "Had the tribal committees been given the chance to work out effective mechanisms ... such conflict might have been averted."[77] Most importantly, local leaders interpreted the government's actions as an infringement of their autonomy and a breach of long-standing agreements between them and the state.[78] Speaking of the military operations in the FATA, a former director general of Inter-Services Intelligence (ISI), Lt. Gen. (Retd.) Asad Durrani, asserted:

> Military action was taken in haste. Regular channels of conflict resolution and dialogue should have taken precedence over the use of military force, which undermined the capacity of the administration and local tribesman.[79]

Another serious blow to the authority of the local leaders happened when the military arrested local tribesmen and stopped paying allowances to the local leaders. For example, the government arrested 13 tribal elders from the Ahmadzai Wazir and 64 other tribesmen in the South Waziristan Agency.[80] In addition, government repressive measures not only included arbitrary arrests, but local leaders were also attacked. For example, on 24 February 2004, the military targeted a gathering of tribal leaders who were set to deliberate on the procedure for expelling foreign fighters.[81] A local official said, "The military arrived armed with helicopter gunships when negotiations were underway...a step that undermined whatever little local trust could be harnessed."[82]

The government also withheld the allowances and privileges of around 349 tribal leaders. The government also stopped paying salaries to those Wazir tribesmen who were employed by the government.[83] Journalist Rahimullah noted, "With the leading *Maliks* [tribal leaders] in jail and their wages stopped, it was obvious that they had been stripped of any power or influence to play a role in defusing the crisis."[84] The government's approach increasingly lost the confidence of the tribal leaders. A Wazir tribal elder said, "We were promised dialogue and developmental funds, while plans for military operations against our tribes were well underway. We were stabbed in the back."[85] The government's militaristic approach followed by extreme actions increasingly alienated the local leaders, thereby providing the leadership necessary for the onset of insurgency. To reiterate, insurgency in FATA erupted when state repression on masses is combined with a disruption of the previous *modus vivendi* centered on co-optation of local elites.

Conclusion

The detailed empirical information supported with the theoretical insights provided in this chapter establishes that the state repression in FATA provided recruits to rebel movement, while the disruption of patronage network of local elites stripping them of shared political power created leadership opportunities for more radical or militant elements who in turn led the movement to take off. At the beginning of 2004, Washington exerted substantial pressure on Pakistan to conduct tough military operations in the FATA because of the alleged security concerns in Afghanistan. The Pakistani military succumbed to the US pressure carried out a number of military operations in the FATA. An indiscriminate use of force by the military resulted in human rights abuses such as civilian causalities and destruction of property which in turn led to widespread public anger at the grassroots level. The necessary leadership for the rebel movement was provided when the government disrupted the longstanding *status quo* while depriving the local leaders of political power and the monetary allowances. This is when insurgency erupted in FATA.

In December 2007, the insurgents operating in different parts of the FATA united to form Tehrik-i-Taliban Pakistan (TTP). Sharing of resources and concerted actions against the Pakistani government allowed the TTP in establishing strong-holds in different parts of FATA. In addition, they also extended their influence in some settled parts of Pakistan, such as Malakand division, which was under the regular control of the government. The next chapter explains that the government's poor counterinsurgency efforts in the following years provided TTP an opportunity to develop into a powerful insurgent force.

Notes

1 Mark Irving Lichbach, "Deterrence or Escalation?: The puzzle of aggregate studies of repression and dissent," *Journal of Conflict Resolution* 31, no 2 (1987);

Lars-Eric Cederman, Simon Hug, and Livia I. Schubiger, "Civilian Victimization and Ethnic Civil War," *Paper prepared for the Annual Meeting of the American Political Science Association*, April 5–8, 2018; Jeff Goodwin, *No Other Way Out: States and Revolutionary Movements, 1945–1991* (Cambridge: Cambridge University Press, 2001); T. David Mason and Dale Krane, "The Political Economy of Death Squads," *International Studies Quarterly* 33, no. 2 (1989): 175–198; Stathis N. Kalyvas and Mathew Kocher, "How 'Free' is the Free-Riding in Civil Wars?," *World Politics* 59, no. 2 (2007): 177–216.

2 Lichbach, "Deterrence or Escalation?."

3 Shehzad H. Qazi, "Rebels of the Frontier: Origins, Organization, and Recruitment of the Pakistani Taliban," *Small Wars & Insurgencies* 22, no. 4 (2011): 574–602; Shuja Nawaz, *FATA – A Most Dangerous Place: Meeting the Challenge of Militancy and Terror in the Federally Administered Tribal Areas of Pakistan* (Washington DC: Center for Strategic & International Studies, 2009); Ashok K. Behuria, "Fighting the Taliban: Pakistan at War with Itself," *Australian Journal of International Affairs* 61, no. 4 (2007): 529–43.

4 Ayaz Wazir, a former ambassador and resident of South Waziristan (Islamabad), interview by author, 4 November 2013.

5 Syed Waqar Ali Shah. *Ethnicity, Islam and Nationalism: Muslim Politics in the North-West Frontier Province 1937–47* (Karachi, Pakistan: Oxford University Press, 1999), 221.

6 Claude Rakisits, "Pakistan's Tribal Areas: A Critical No-Man's Land," in *Identity and Conflict*, ed. A. Vautravers and E. James (Geneva: Webster University, 2008), 128.

7 James William Spain, *The Pathan Borderland* (Hague: Mouton & Co, 1963), 145.

8 Rashid Ahmad Khan, "FATA After Independence: 1947–2001," in *Federally Administered Tribal Areas of Pakistan*, ed. Noor ul Haq, Rashid Ahmad Khan, and Maqsudul Hasan Nuri (Islamabad: Islamabad Policy Research Institute), 2005

9 Jinnah's Address to the Tribal Jirga at Government House, Peshawar, April 17, 1948. *Quaid-I-Azam Mohammad Ali Jinnah Speeches and Statements as Governor General of Pakistan 1947–48* (Islamabad: Ministry of Information & Broadcasting Directorate of Films & Publications, 1989), 238–39

10 *Quaid-I-Azam Mohammad Ali Jinnah Speeches and Statements as Governor General of Pakistan 1947–48, 239*

11 Gul Khan Marjan, local leader in South Waziristan, interview by author, 22 February 2014.

12 Ahmad Khan, "FATA After Independence," 27.

13 Nawaz, *FATA – A Most Dangerous Place,* 8.

14 Muhammad Maqbool Khan Wazir, "Geopolitics of FATA After 9/11," *IPRI Journal* XI, no. 1 (2011): 59–76. Ayaz Wazir, "Will FATA Ever Be Developed?," *The News*, March 17, 2012.

15 Adnan Naseemullah, "Shades of Sovereignty: Explaining Political Order and Disorder in Pakistan's Northwest," *Studies in Comparative International Development* 49 (2014): 501–522.

16 Naseemullah, "Shades of Sovereignty."

17 Lt. Gen. Ali Jan Orakzai, former Corps Commander Peshawar and Governor Khyber Pakhtunkhwa (Rawalpindi), interview by author, 5 April 2014.

18 Lt. Gen. Ali Jan Orakzai interview.

19 Jonathan Goodhand, "Enduring Disorder and Persistent Poverty: A Review of the Linkages Between War and Chronic Poverty," *World Development* 31, no. 3 (2003): 629–646.

20 David D. Laitin, *Nations, States and Violence* (Oxford: Oxford University Press, 2007), 23; James D. Fearon, "Governance and Civil War Onset," *World Development Report* (2011).

21 Andreas Foro Tollefsen, and Halvard Buhaug. "Insurgency and Inaccessibility," *International Studies Review* 17 (2015): 6–25; Paul Collier, Anke Hoeffler, Dominic Rohner, "Beyond Greed and Grievance: Feasibility and Civil War," *Oxford Economic Papers* 61, no. 1 (2009): 1–27.
22 Cederman et al., "Civilian Victimization and Ethnic Civil War,"; Jeff Goodwin, *No Other Way Out: States and Revolutionary Movements, 1945–1991* (Cambridge: Cambridge University Press, 2001).
23 Elisabeth Jean Wood, *Insurgent Collective Action and Civil War in El Salvador* (New York: Cambridge University Press, 2003), 116.
24 Stathis N. Kalyvas and Mathew Kocher, "How 'Free' is the Free-Riding in Civil Wars?," *World Politics* 59, no. 2 (2007): 177–216.
25 Jeff Goodwin, *No Other Way Out: States and Revolutionary Movements, 1945–1991*.
26 Lichbach, "Deterrence or Escalation?,": 266.
27 Cederman et al., "Civilian Victimization and Ethnic Civil War."
28 Luke N. Condra and Jabob N. Shapiro, "Who Takes the Blame?: The Strategic Effects of Collateral Damage," *American Journal of Political Science* 56, no. 1 (2012): 167–187.
29 Joseph Young, "Repression, Dissent and the Onset of Civil War: States, Dissidents and the production of Violent Conflict" (PhD Thesis, Florida State University Libraries, 2008), 518.
30 Many Al Qaeda militants hide themselves in big cities such as Karachi, Lahore, Faisalabad and other parts of Pakistan including the tribal areas. The Pakistani local law enforcement agencies had arrested hundreds of Al Qaeda suspects since the launch of the US-led anti-terror campaign in Afghanistan. Of these, 480 were handed over to the US authorities. Khalid Shaikh Mohammad was the highest-ranking Al Qaeda operative apprehended by the Pakistani security forces. Abu Zubaydah, Al Qaeda's chief of operations, was nabbed in Faisalabad. And Ramzi Bin Al-Shaiba, a Yemeni believed to be a chief planner in the September 11 attacks was arrested from Karachi. Qudssia Akhlaque, "480 Al Qaeda Men Handed over to US," *Dawn*, March 11, 2003; "Pakistan Takes Hunt for Al Qaeda into Cities," *Daily Times*, October 30, 2002.
31 Khalid Hasan, "Pakistani Security Setup Not Fully Cooperative: Armitage," *Daily Times*, October 2, 2003.
32 Rahimullah Yusufzai,"Internationally Administered Trouble Areas." *The News*, October 12, 2003.
33 Anwar Iqbal, "New Operation Launched in Tribal Areas," *Dawn*, February 18, 2004.
34 "25 Nabbed in Wana Operation," *The Nation*, February 25, 2004.
35 Zahid Hussain, *Frontline Pakistan* (London: I.B. Tauris&Co, 2007), 147.
36 Anwar Iqbal, "New Operations Launched." *Dawn*, February 18, 2004.
37 Shabana Fayyaz, "Towards a Durable Peace in Waziristan," *Pakistan Security Research Unit*, Brief No. 10, 2007
38 "Fighting Intensifies in S. Waziristan," *Dawn*, September 15, 2004.
39 Ali Wazir, an elder of South Waziristan (Peshawar), interview by author, 26 January, 2014.
40 Rahimullah Yusufzai, "Army Launches Operation against Al-Qaeda in Wana," *The News*, 2004.
41 Ali Wazir, an elder of South Waziristan (Peshawar), interview by author, 26 January 2014. Gohar Mehsud, a resident of South Waziristan (Islamabad), interview by author, 20 April 2014, and Ali Wazir, a local leader from South Waziristan (Peshawar), interview by author, 26 January 2014. 56.
42 Gohar Mehsud, a resident of South Waziristan (Islamabad), interview by author, 20 April 2014, and Ali Wazir, a local leader from South Waziristan (Peshawar), interview by author, 26 January 2014. 56.

43 Rustam Shah Mohmand, a former political agent in FATA (Peshawar), interview by author, 20 February, 2014.

44 Ismail Khan, "Army Winding up Operation: Corps Commander," *Dawn*, March 26, 2004.

45 Rahimullah Yusufzai and Sailab Mahsud, "Fighting Subsides as Jirga Seeks Truce," *The News*, March 22, 2004.

46 Amnesty International. "Pakistan: Human Rights Abuses in Search for Al-Qa'ida and Taleban in the Tribal Areas." April 2004. https://www.amnesty.org/download/Documents/96000/asa330112004en.pdf.

47 Ismail Khan and Baqir Sajjad Syed, "Airstrikes Launched in Shakai," *Dawn*, June 12, 2004.

48 Yusufzai and Mahsud, "Fighting Subsides as Jirga Seeks Truce."

49 Zulfiqar Ali, "17 Foreign Militants Killed in Gunbattle: Operation in N. Waziristan," *Dawn*, July 18, 2005.

50 Behroz Khan, "20 Arrested in Wana Operation: Detainees Include Saudis, Egyptians, Yemenis," *The News*, February 25, 2004.

51 "Operation in Waziristan," *Dawn*, June 17, 2004.

52 Pazir Gul, "N. Waziristan Tribesmen Observe Strike," *Dawn*, September 1, 2004.

53 Shamim Shahid, "Jirga Demands Troops out," *The Nation*, April 8, 2006.

54 Rahimullah Yusufzai, "80 Die in Air Attack on Bajaur Seminary," *The News*, October 31, 2006.

55 "HRW Warns against Excessive Use of Force," *The News*, November 2, 2006.

56 Amnesty International, *Pakistan: Human Rights Abuses in the Search for Al-Qa'ida and Taleban in the Tribal Areas*, Report, April 2004.

57 Rahimullah Yusufzai, "Bajaur Elders Were Ready to Rein in Militants," *The News*, November 2, 2006.

58 "Economic Blockade of South Waziristan Termed Violation of Human Rights," *The News*, June 6, 2004.

59 Rahimullah Yusufzai, "Wana: Internal Imbargo," *The News*, June 6, 2004

60 Rahimullah Yusufzai, "Issue: Another Truce," February 13, 2005.

61 Shaiq Hussain and Haq Nawaz, "Local Taliban Gaining Strength in NWA," *The Nation*, March 14, 2006.

62 "Avoiding Over-Reaction," *The Nation*, July 19, 2005.

63 Rahimullah Yusufzai, "Security: After the 'End,'" *The News*, June 20, 2004.

64 Hassan Abbas, "Militancy in Pakistan's Borderland: Implications for the Nation and for Afghan Policy," *Century Foundation Report* (2010), 15.

65 Syeda Beena Butool, "Pakistani Responses to AfPak Policy Local Narratives and an Ending Global War?," *Asian Survey* 53, no. 6 (2013): 1018.

66 Aldon D. Morris and Suzanne Staggenbourg. "Leadership in Social Movements," in *The Blackwell Companion to Social Movements,* eds. David A. Snow, et al. (Malden, MA, US: Blackwell Publishing, 2004), 171.

67 Vasanjit Banerjee, "The Religious Origins of Class Coalitions: Elite Participation in Religiously Motivated Peasant Rebellions in Mexico, Zimbabwe, and India," *International Political Science Review* 36, no. 5 (2014): 547–8.

68 Hanne Fjelde and Indra De Soysa. "Coercion, Co-optation, or Cooperation?: State capacity and the Risk of Civil War, 1961–2004," *Conflict Management and Peace Science* 26, no. 1 (2009): 5–25.

69 Jack A. Goldstone, *Revolutions: A Very Short Introduction* (New York: Oxford University Press, 2014), 13.

70 Margaret Levi, "Why We Need a New Theory of Government." *Perspective on Politics* 4, no. 1 (2006): 5–19

71 Ted Robert Gurr, "Why Minorities Rebel: A Global Analysis of Communal Mobilization and Conflict Since 1945," *International Political Science Review* 14, no. 2 (1993): 178.

22   *Repression, Co-optation and Insurgency*

72 David S. Siroky and John Cuffe, "Lost Autonomy, Nationalism and Separatism," *Comparative Political Studies* 48, no.1 (2015): 5.
73 Cite in Naseemullah, "Shades of Sovereignty," 517.
74 Butool, "Pakistani Responses to AfPak," 1016.
75 Rahimullah Yusufzai, "Militancy: All That Ends Well," *The News*, May 2, 2004.
76 Rohan Gunaratna and Syed Adnan Ali Shah Bukhari, "Making peace with Pakistan Taliban to isolate Al-Qaeda: Success and Failures," *Peace and Security Review* 1 (2008): 1–25.
77 Butool, "Pakistani Responses to AfPak Policy," 1019.
78 Khalid Aziz, former political agent in FATA, interview by author (Peshawar), 10 January 2014.
79 Cited in International Crisis Group, *Pakistan's Tribal Areas: Appeasing the Militants* (ICG: Brussels, 2006), 15.
80 "Wana Bazaar Sealed, More Tribesmen Held," *The News*, May 31, 2004.
81 Butool, "Pakistani Responses to AfPak Policy," 1016.
82 Cited in Group, *Pakistan's Tribal Areas*, 15.
83 International Crisis Group, *Pakistan's Tribal Areas*, 15.
84 Yusufzai, "Wana: Internal Imbargo."
85 Cited in Group, *Pakistan's Tribal Areas*, 14.

Bibliography

Abbas, Hassan. "Militancy in Pakistan's Borderland: Implications for the Nation and for Afghan Policy." *Century Foundation Report*, 2010.
Ahmad Khan, Rashid. "FATA After Independence: 1947–2001." In *Federally Administered Tribal Areas of Pakistan*, edited by Noor ul Haq, Rashid Ahmad Khan, and Maqsudul Hasan Nuri. Islamabad: Islamabad Policy Research Institute, 2005.
Ali, Zulfiqar. "17 Foreign Militants Killed in Gunbattle: Operation in N. Waziristan." *Dawn*, July 18, 2005.
Amnesty International. *Pakistan: Human Rights Abuses in the Search for Al-Qa'ida and Taleban in the Tribal Areas*, Report, April2004. Accessed on June 12, 2020. https://www.amnesty.org/download/Documents/96000/asa330112004en.pdf.
"Avoiding Over-Reaction." *The Nation*, July 19, 2005.
Banerjee, Vasanjit. "The Religious Origins of Class Coalitions: Elite Participation in Religiously Motivated Peasant Rebellions in Mexico, Zimbabwe, and India." *International Political Science Review* 36, no. 5 (2014): 545–561.
Behuria, Ashok K. "Fighting the Taliban: Pakistan at War with Itself." *Australian Journal of International Affairs* 61, no. 4 (2007): 529–543.
Butool, Syeda Beena. "Pakistani Responses to AfPak Policy Local Narratives and an Ending Global War?." *Asian Survey* 53, no. 6 (2013): 1005–1036.
Cederman, Lars-Eric, Simon Hug, and Livia I.Schubiger. "Civilian Victimization and Ethnic Civil War." *Paper prepared for the Annual Meeting of the American Political Science Association*, April 5–8, 2018.
Collier, Paul, Anke Hoeffler, and Dominic Rohner. "Beyond Greed and Grievance: Feasibility and Civil War." *Oxford Economic Papers* 61, no. 1 (2009): 1–27.
Condra, Luke N., and Jabob N.Shapiro, "Who Takes the Blame?: The Strategic Effects of Collateral Damage." *American Journal of Political Science* 56, no. 1 (2012): 167–187.
"Economic Blockade of South Waziristan Termed Violation of Human Rights." *The News*, June 6, 2004.

Fayyaz, Shabana. "Towards a Durable Peace in Waziristan." *Pakistan Security Research Unit*, Brief No. 10, 2007.

"Fighting Intensifies in S. Waziristan." *Dawn*, September 15, 2004.

Fearon, James D. "Governance and Civil War Onset." *World Development Report* (2011).

Fjelde, Hanne, and Indra De Soysa. "Coercion, Co-optation, or Cooperation?: State capacity and the Risk of Civil War, 1961–2004." *Conflict Management and Peace Science* 26, no. 1 (2009): 5–25.

Foro Tollefsen, Andreas, and Halvard Buhaug. "Insurgency and Inaccessibility." *International Studies Review* 17 (2015): 6–25.

"480 Al Qaeda Men Handed over to US." *Dawn*, March 11, 2003.

Goldstone, Jack A. *Revolutions: A Very Short Introduction*. New York: Oxford University Press, 2014.

Goodhand, Jonathan. "Enduring Disorder and Persistent Poverty: A Review of the Linkages Between War and Chronic Poverty." *World Development* 31, no. 3 (2003): 629–646.

Goodwin, Jeff. *No Other Way Out: States and Revolutionary Movements, 1945–1991*. Cambridge: Cambridge University Press, 2001.

Gul, Pazir. "N. Waziristan Tribesmen Observe Strike." *Dawn*, September 1, 2004.

Gunaratna, Rohan, and Syed Adnan Ali Shah Bukhari. "Making peace with Pakistan Taliban to isolate Al-Qaeda: Success and Failures." *Peace and Security Review* 1 (2008): 1–25.

Gurr, Ted Robert. "Why Minorities Rebel: A Global Analysis of Communal Mobilization and Conflict Since 1945." *International Political Science Review* 14, no. 2 (1993): 161–201.

Hasan, Khalid. "Pakistani Security Setup Not Fully Cooperative: Armitage." *Daily Times*, October 2, 2003.

"HRW Warns against Excessive Use of Force." *The News*, November 2, 2006.

Hussain, Shaiq, and Haq Nawaz. "Local Taliban Gaining Strength in NWA." *The Nation*, March 14, 2006.

Hussain, Zahid. *Frontline Pakistan*. London: I.B. Tauris&Co, 2007.

International Crisis Group. *Pakistan's Tribal Areas: Appeasing the Militants*. Brussels: ICG, 2006.

Iqbal, Anwar. "New Operation Launched in Tribal Areas." *Dawn*, February 18, 2004.

Kalyvas, Stathis N., and Mathew Kocher. "How 'Free' is the Free-Riding in Civil Wars?." *World Politics* 59, no. 2 (2007): 177–216.

Khan, Behroz. "20 Arrested in Wana Operation: Detainees Include Saudis, Egyptians, Yemenis." *The News*, February 25, 2004.

Khan, Ismail. "Army Winding up Operation: Corps Commander." *Dawn*, March 26, 2004.

Khan, Ismail, and Baqir Sajjad Syed. "Airstrikes Launched in Shakai." *Dawn*, June 12, 2004.

Laitin, David D. *Nations, States and Violence*. Oxford: Oxford University Press, 2007.

Levi, Margaret. "Why We Need a New Theory of Government." *Perspective on Politics* 4, no. 1 (2006): 5–19.

Lichbach, Mark Irving. "Deterrence or Escalation?: The puzzle of aggregate studies of repression and dissent," *Journal of Conflict Resolution* 31, no 2 (1987): 266–297.

Maqbool Khan Wazir, Muhammad. "Geopolitics of FATA After 9/11." *IPRI Journal XI*, no. 1 (2011): 59–76.

Mason, T. David, and Dale Krane. "The Political Economy of Death Squads." *International Studies Quarterly* 33, no. 2 (1989): 175–198.

Ministry of Information & Broadcasting. *Quaid-I-Azam Mohammad Ali Jinnah Speeches and Statements as Governor General of Pakistan 1947–48.* Islamabad: Ministry of Information & Broadcasting Directorate of Films & Publications, 1989.

Morris, Aldon D., and Suzanne Staggenbourg. "Leadership in Social Movements." In *The Blackwell Companion to Social Movements,* edited by David A.Snow, Sarah A. Soule, and Hanspeter Kriesi. Malden, MA: Blackwell Publishing, 2004.

Naseemullah, Adnan. "Shades of Sovereignty: Explaining Political Order and Disorder in Pakistan's Northwest." *Studies in Comparative International Development* 49 (2014): 501–522.

Nawaz, Shuja. *FATA - A Most Dangerous Place: Meeting the Challenge of Militancy and Terror in the Federally Administered Tribal Areas of Pakistan.* Washington DC: Center for Strategic & International Studies, 2009.

"Operation in Waziristan." *Dawn,* June 17, 2004.

"Pakistan Takes Hunt for Al Qaeda into Cities." *Daily Times,* October 30, 2002.

Qazi, Shehzad H. "Rebels of the Frontier: Origins, Organization, and Recruitment of the Pakistani Taliban." *Small Wars & Insurgencies* 22, no. 4 (2011): 574–602.

Rakisits, Claude. "Pakistan's Tribal Areas: A Critical No-Man's Land." In *Identity and Conflict,* edited by A. Vautravers and E. James. Geneva: Webster University, 2008.

Shahid, Shamim. "Jirga Demands Troops out." *The Nation,* April 8, 2006.

Siroky, David S. and John Cuffe. "Lost Autonomy, Nationalism and Separatism." *Comparative Political Studies* 48, no.1 (2015): 3–34.

Spain, James William. *The Pathan Borderland.* Hague: Mouton & Co, 1963.

"Wana Bazaar Sealed, More Tribesmen Held." *The News,* May 31, 2004.

Waqar Ali Shah, Syed. *Ethnicity, Islam and Nationalism: Muslim Politics in the North-West Frontier Province 1937–47.* Karachi, Pakistan: Oxford University Press, 1999.

Wood, Elisabeth Jean. *Insurgent Collective Action and Civil War in El Salvador.* New York: Cambridge University Press, 2003.

Young, Joseph. "Repression, Dissent and the Onset of Civil War: States, Dissidents and the production of Violent Conflict." PhD Thesis, Florida State University Libraries, 2008.

Yusufzai, Rahimullah. "Internationally Administered Trouble Areas." *The News,* October 12, 2003.

Yusufzai, Rahimullah. "Army Launches Operation against Al-Qaeda in Wana." *The News,* 2004.

Yusufzai, Rahimullah, and Sailab Mahsud, "Fighting Subsides as Jirga Seeks Truce." *The News,* March 22, 2004.

Yusufzai, Rahimullah. "Militancy: All That Ends Well." *The News,* May 2, 2004.

Yusufzai, Rahimullah. "Security: After the 'End'." *The News,* June 20, 2004.

Yusufzai, Rahimullah. "Wana: Internal Imbargo." *The News,* June 6, 2004.

Yusufzai, Rahimullah. "Issue: Another Truce." February 13, 2005.

Yusufzai, Rahimullah. "Bajaur Elders Were Ready to Rein in Militants." *The News,* November 2, 2006.

Yusufzai, Rahimullah. "80 Die in Air Attack on Bajaur Seminary." *The News,* October 31, 2006.

3 Weak Counterinsurgency and the Rise of the FATA Insurgency

This chapter argues that a poor counterinsurgency strategy by the Pakistani government allowed the FATA insurgency to grow. The insurgents not only succeeded in extending their control over the most parts of FATA, but they also vied for influence in the settled areas of Pakistan such as Swat. This chapter discusses the various constituents of the Pakistani government's counterinsurgency strategy and how this led to the escalation of the FATA insurgency. The theoretical literature guides the analysis of the deficiencies in the government's counterinsurgency approach. Firstly, the chapter elaborates how a lack of political will on the part of the Pakistani government undermined the seriousness of the insurgency threat and lacked devising an appropriate response to tackle the problem. The chapter argues further that instead of developing a counterinsurgency doctrine and relevant skills, the Pakistani government mainly relied on the conventional forces in fighting the insurgency that proved counterproductive. The chapter then turns to discuss how insufficient or incompetent local security forces, who were unable to defend the local population, allowed the insurgents to gain a foothold of the territory. Finally, the chapter contends that the Pakistani government's strategy of conducting negotiations with insurgents from a position of weakness after failed military operations not only allowed the latter to gain legitimacy in the eyes of the local population but also helped them secure popular support, mostly through coercive means, to extend their influence. A combination of these misguided approaches explains the rise of the FATA insurgency.

Formation of the TTP and the Growing Insurgent Threat

Several small and disparate militant groups operating in different parts of the FATA coalesced to form Tehrik-e-Taliban Pakistan (TTP) in December 2007, under the leadership of the South Waziristan-based Baitullah Mehsud. After the TTP's formation, the insurgents not only succeeded in establishing a stronghold in the FATA, but also projected their influence into the settled parts of the country adjacent to the tribal areas. For example, in April 2009 an affiliated group of the TTP took control of Buner, a key district in the

DOI: 10.4324/9781003349259-3

Malakkand division located in the environs of the Swat Valley, approximately only 170 kilometres away from Islamabad, the capital of Pakistan.[1] This unsurprisingly generated serious concerns within Pakistan, and also in the United States, that the insurgents might gain access to Pakistan's 60–100 nuclear weapons.[2]

The establishment of the TTP marked the real onset of insurgency against the Pakistani state. There was an escalation of insurgent attacks on the security forces. A month after the establishment of the TTP, the group attacked the Sararogha Fort in South Waziristan, killing scores of security personnel and capturing the fort.[3] The militants also ambushed a convoy of paramilitary FC forces, killing 22 soldiers, in the Loisam area of Bajaur Agency.[4] In another instance, Baitullah-led militants captured 242 Pakistani soldiers in an ambush in South Waziristan. This was regarded as the most humiliating moment for the Pakistani army thus far.[5] The military later recovered these soldiers, but only after the reciprocal release of 24 militants, some of whom had been convicted of planning suicide bombings. "This was a bitter pill that we had to swallow", one senior military officer later said.[6] The TTP was emboldened by its achievements and proclaimed in 2008 they would take the war out of the tribal areas into the rest of Pakistan. A statement by the TTP read: "we [TTP] will take this war out of tribal areas and NWFP to the rest of the country and will attack security forces and important government functionaries in Islamabad, Lahore, Karachi and other big cities."[7]

The empirical evidence in the remainder of this chapter demonstrates that a range of poor counterinsurgency steps by the Pakistani government and military provided ample opportunities to the insurgency to grow.

Pakistan's Weak Counterinsurgency in the FATA

The TTP's growth in size and strength can be largely ascribed to an ineffective or poor counterinsurgency strategy by the Pakistani government from 2004 to 2008.[8] Arguably, various constituents of Pakistan's counterinsurgency strategy rendered the campaign a failure. At first, the Pakistani government of General Pervaz Musharaf joined the US-led "war on terror" under pressure from Washington as well as its own strategic compulsions, mainly centered on India.[9] Therefore, in the first few years, the Pakistani government largely viewed it as an American war.[10] The majority of the Pakistani public also doubted whether the country was fighting its own war.[11] Most importantly, until around 2009, the government did not see the FATA insurgency as a critical threat to Pakistan's national security.[12] Therefore, there was a lack of clarity and commitment on the part of the Pakistani government in fighting the Taliban insurgency, which allowed the movement to gain a foothold.

The use of conventional forces by the Pakistani government in fighting the insurgency proved counterproductive. Pakistani military forces were largely trained to fight a conventional war with its archrival, India. And military elites did not show any serious interest in providing counterinsurgency training to the forces fighting the insurgency. Instead, they kept their conventional capabilities intact because of their persistent focus on a conflict with India.[13] David Kilcullen contends that Pakistan's counterinsurgency failed largely due to the conventional nature of the force, which seriously lacked counterinsurgency training and equipment.[14] The conventional and indiscriminate use of military force caused extensive civilian damage, which facilitated the insurgents' recruitment process from the affected population.

Resultantly, the conventional forces failed in uprooting the insurgents. And after the failure of these military ventures, the Pakistani government held peace negotiations with the insurgents, boosting their legitimacy. The government then signed various peace deals with the insurgents, clearly negotiating from a position of weakness, which only boosted the insurgents' strength and confidence in their ability and power. The poorly planned counterinsurgency enabled the FATA insurgency to grow and develop into a powerful movement.

Lack of Political Will

Political will plays an important role in making a counterinsurgency campaign successful.[15] Political will is demonstrated by how the government deals with insurgency at strategic and operational levels, which requires the appropriation of sufficient resources. Dixon notes that a strong political will with clear goals is indispensable to succeed against an insurgency.[16] In addition, if the government demonstrates "the will, the means, and the ability to win" against the insurgents, peoples' support will be forthcoming.[17] For instance, if the people perceive the counterinsurgents as lacking strong will, it is very unlikely that the local people oppose insurgents.[18]

The Pakistani government lacked a strong political will which provided the insurgency with the opportunity to grow. This lack of clarity and commitment in fighting against the terrorism was discernible from the state's motivation to join the US-led war on terrorism. At first, Pakistan was quite reluctant to join the US coalition in Afghanistan against the Taliban forces. The decision was ultimately taken under duress because the military regime realised that any refusal to comply with the US demands would risk Pakistan itself becoming a target state.[19] Moreover, India also appeared to be another crucial factor in Pakistan's decision to be part of the international coalition. Bruce Riedel, contended, "The decision to reverse a decade of Pakistani policy in Afghanistan was a result of the underlying Pakistani concern about India."[20] Even President Musharaf mentioned India while explaining Pakistan's decision to align with the United States.[21] He stated:

I also analyzed our national interest. First, India had already tried to step in by offering its bases to the US. If we did not join the US, it would accept India's offer. What would happen then? India would gain a golden opportunity with regard to Kashmir... . Second, the security of our strategic assets would be jeopardized. We did not want to lose or damage the military parity that we had achieved with India by becoming a nuclear weapons state.[22]

Furthermore, US financial and military assistance greatly induced Pakistan to side with them. To reward and entice Pakistani cooperation, Washington removed economic sanctions inflicted on Pakistan because of the 1998 nuclear tests and the military take-over in 1999. In addition, under the Economic Support Fund (ESF), the United States reduced Pakistan's bilateral debt by US$1 billion in the 2003 financial year (FY) and US$460 million in FY 2004.[23] Moreover, the United States rewarded Pakistan with US$3 billion in cash support and another US$3 billion of loans were written off.[24] The United States also rescheduled Pakistan's debt of $12.5 billion dollars for the next 38 years.[25] Pakistan also received substantial US military assistance through the Foreign Military Financing (FMF) programmes and the Coalition Support Fund (CSF). However, a large portion of this assistance was spent by Pakistan on the procurement of major US weapons systems.[26] Pakistan thereby emerged as one of the largest recipients of US assistance. The United States designated Pakistan as a "major non-NATO ally" (MNNA) of the United States in June 2004.[27] This act allowed Pakistan to access a range of military and financial benefits.

As stated earlier, financial as well as strategic interests primarily motivated Pakistan to join the United States-led coalition in Afghanistan. As a result, the government was less inclined to pursue terrorists with real intent. To put it simply, the Pakistan military had taken actions against the militants hiding in the tribal areas, but these measures were lacking in sincerity and serious intent. Based on the strategic utility of some militant groups, the Pakistani military continued to distinguish among militant groups operating in the FATA. For instance, the Pakistani military targeted some groups especially Al Qaeda and other foreign militants but spared some other groups such as the Afghan Taliban and their local affiliates. In addition, most US military aid was spent on purchasing weapons used for conventional warfare, not for counterinsurgency. A renowned expert on the FATA, Ahmed Rashid, stated, "More than 80 percent of the $10 billion in United States aid to Pakistan since the Sept. 11 attacks has gone to the military; much of it has been used to buy expensive weapons systems for the Indian front rather than the smaller items needed for counterinsurgency."[28]

Even Pakistan's security agencies were believed to have sympathy for some groups whom they considered useful for fighting in Afghanistan and Kashmir.[29] An expert, Seth Jones, asserted, "Not only did Pakistan refuse to target some militant organizations, but some elements in the ISI, Frontier Corps, and military continued to back some of them."[30] Some US officials alleged that Pakistan's intelligence agency (ISI) had provided support to some militant groups that attacked the United States-led forces in Afghanistan; although, the Pakistani government refuted these contentions.[31] Aqil Shah maintained:

> While the military and other security agencies have cooperated with the United States against al-Qaeda fugitives, the security establishment's track record when it comes to controlling the Pakistani and Afghan Taliban has been less encouraging. Whatever resolve the military might harbor to deal firmly with the Pakistani and Afghan Taliban is trumped by the army's perceived need to retain ties to the Taliban as an insurance policy against Indian influence in Afghanistan.[32]

This practice of targeting some groups and leaving others undermined the government's ability to establish the state's writ in its entirety. Maj. Gen. Athar Abbas, former Director General of Inter-services Public Relations (ISPR), acknowledged that Pakistan's discriminatory approach towards various militant groups in the FATA ultimately helped the insurgency to grow stronger.[33]

Pakistan's security forces also lacked motivation to fight the insurgency because of a lack of public support. Many Pakistanis, especially the tribal people, opposed Pakistan's alliance with the United States and considered the military's raids in the FATA as part of an "American war."[34] Lacking larger public support, the security forces appeared demoralised and unwilling to fight their countrymen. For instance, some 250 Pakistani army and paramilitary troops surrendered to the insurgents without a fight in South Waziristan.[35] A local resident of Bajaur Agency explained how this state of affairs led to the growing power of the insurgents:

> They [insurgents] burnt schools, destroyed hospitals, and by doing this they completely destroyed the places which were for the benefit of the people... The government was watching everything that the militants were doing, including destroying security forces pickets, roads, and bridges. But the government didn't do anything. Then Bajaur Agency became completely under the control of the Taleban. Even then the government didn't do anything.[36]

At the beginning of the counterinsurgency campaign, the paramilitary Frontier Corps (FC), predominantly Pashtun, was at the forefront of fighting the insurgency because of their local knowledge of the terrain and customs. The FC soldiers had ethnic ties with the local insurgents that bound them more tightly to the tribesmen than to the Punjabi military forces. Unsurprisingly, when the FC was used in the earlier phases of counterinsurgency operations, "it suffered from large-scale desertion, surrender and loss of morale."[37]

Furthermore, due to the absence of strong will, the counterinsurgency campaign was largely inconsistent in its response to the growing insurgency.

Jones explained the weaknesses of Pakistan's initial counterinsurgency operations: "Pakistan's operations were not sustained over time. Pakistani efforts were marked by sweeps, searches, and occasional bloody battles, but none of these employed enough forces to hold territory."[38] In addition, the Pakistani government's repeatedly accommodating policies towards the insurgents exhibited a lack of seriousness. Up until late 2008, even after the establishment of the TTP in December 2007, the Pakistani government did not see the FATA insurgency as a serious challenge to the state.

While Pakistani officials were well aware of the insurgents' advances in establishing a parallel authority in the FATA, they largely viewed the insurgency as a "threat to be contained, not defeated."[39] Military actions against the FATA insurgents were usually "incomplete, inconclusive and, at times, appeared insincere."[40] Moreover, a lack of coordination between multiple security agencies, including regular army units, the paramilitary Frontier Corps as well as military intelligence agencies, also undermined the operation. "It seems like every agency is running its own shop with constant back and forth from the corps commander to the governor and back", said Brig. (Retd.) A.R. Siddiqi.[41]

Fighting Insurgency Employing Conventional Forces

A conventional force is quite incapable of fighting insurgency because counterinsurgency warfare is qualitatively different from conventional warfare. Frank Kitson argued that "The qualities required for fighting conventional war are different from those required for dealing with subversion or insurgency."[42] Fighting insurgency through conventional force may cause great military losses, because it hardly distinguishes between common people and insurgents, which may potentially result in serious damage to the civilian population and create more grievances against government forces. This can potentially harm the counterinsurgency campaign.

A transformation of conventional forces into counterinsurgency ones is considered imperative in subduing an insurgency, however it is not without challenge. Roger Trinuier contended that the French counterinsurgency operations in Indochina and Algeria failed primarily because of the French forces' failure to adapt to becoming a counterinsurgency force.[43] Similarly, John Nagl attributed the British army's success in counterinsurgency in Malaya to its rapid learning of counterinsurgency techniques, whereas the failure of America's counterinsurgency in Vietnam was associated with its inability to learn the techniques of counterinsurgency warfare.[44]

The Pakistan Government's initial counterinsurgency campaign in fighting the FATA insurgency mainly relied on the conventional forces that failed to get the desired results. The Pakistani army has long maintained a conventional force posture that was primarily trained and equipped to fight a conventional war with India.[45] Previous wars with India had involved operations across the plains of Punjab. Therefore, Pakistan's army was ill-prepared for counterinsurgency warfare. An observer of the FATA insurgency, Aqil, affirmed that "trained for a conventional war with India, the army was ill-equipped to wage a counterinsurgency campaign."[46]

To adapt to counterinsurgency warfare, a major reorientation was needed in Pakistan's strategic thinking which had traditionally put India as the country's main security threat. Moreover, it dictated a change in arms procurement policies and reform in the military's curriculum.[47] However, the Pakistani military remained quite reluctant in changing its forces' orientation from a conventional to a counterinsurgency force. A consistent fear of a superior Indian army and lack of resources explain this reluctance. The then chief of army staff, Gen. Ashfaq Kayani even refused offers from the US military and NATO officials to retrain or reequip troops to fight the counterinsurgency war. He stated that the bulk of the army would remain deployed along the eastern border to defend Pakistan against its arch-rival India.[48] Likewise, Sameer explained that the Pakistani military's inability to adapt to counterinsurgency was "because of its sheer difficulty, [and due to] the prohibitive costs in money and manpower, organizational lags, and substantial trade-offs with Pakistani grand strategy and military doctrine."[49] A US intelligence assessment noted the Pakistani military' lack of preparedness in fighting the insurgency successfully. A US Defence Intelligence Assessment (DIA) concluded:

> Pakistan lacks the transport and attack helicopters and upgraded communication gear needed to prosecute more effective and sophisticated counter-insurgency operations. Much of the Pakistani army also lacks the knowledge and language skills required to successfully operate across the tribal frontier's complicated cultural terrain.[50]

Furthermore, locally recruited paramilitary Frontier Corps (FC) forces initially spearheaded the fight with the insurgents because of the sensitivity of the Pashtun towards the deployment of regular troops from the pre-dominantly ethnic Punjabi army. As discussed above, the FC was therefore poorly motivated because of this ethnic factor.[51] They also seriously lacked training and modern weapons. The US Defence Intelligence Agency (DIA) assessment noted, "Frontier Corps troops understand the culture and region better and speak the local language, they have even less equipment and less training than the military."[52] Samarjit Ghosh noted that the conventional army of Pakistan, equipped with tanks and artillery and aided by aircrafts, was inept at fighting against the insurgents who were skilled in guerrilla warfare.[53] There were high casualties amongst both the army and the Frontier Corps because of their inadequate counterinsurgency skills. For example, the army lost hundreds of soldiers during military operations in the FATA in 2004.[54] A Western estimate also claimed that the Pakistani military lost 70 percent of its battles with the insurgents.[55] Ghosh explained the causes of these failures, as such:

Nobody can expect soldiers and their leaders to be instant experts in all types of warfare. Fighting through such terrain demands very different skills to those required in an armored advance. These skills can be acquired, but not overnight; it was extremely unwise to commit troops to footslogging, ambush-prone, classic frontier warfare without extensive and lengthy preparation.[56]

Indiscriminate Use of Force

Fighting insurgency through repressive measures can potentially make the population hostile to the counterinsurgents. Most importantly, indiscriminate or excessive use of force in a counterinsurgency campaign is highly counter-productive. Frank Kitson contended that the indiscriminate use of force tends to alienate civilian populations and can potentially harm the counter-insurgency campaign.[57] Jeremy Weinstein argued further, "Indiscriminate violence can drive civilians into the waiting arms of rebel groups ... Extreme levels of state violence often leaves civilians no other option than to join the insurgents."[58] Another expert, Zaidi, affirms this view, "The myopic use of a firepower-intensive approach is a classic flaw in counter-insurgency campaigns, and its indiscriminate use uniquely alienates the target audience."[59] In a similar vein, Constantin Melnik argued that "It is necessary to eliminate the negative feelings on which the insurgency is based. However, the use of force and violence runs the risk of increasing these same negative feelings."[60]

With a traditional outlook focused solely on fighting a conventional war against India aimed at pysical destruction and military infrastructure, the Pakistani army adopted an improvised strategy to deal with the insurgency.[61] No efforts were made to change the forces' orientation towards counter-insurgency practices. Seriously lacking skills and experience in counter-insurgency operations, Pakistan's military mainly relied on heavy use of force to counter insurgency and that proved counterproductive.[62] Zaidi maintained that, "Conventional warfare has tended to shape the trajectories of Pakistani COIN operations, which had proved unsuccessful."[63] Similarly, David Kilcullen maintained that in challenging the insurgency the Pakistani army "applied a heavily 'kinetic', firepower-based approach," i.e. heavy use of airpower and artillery.[64]

An indiscriminate use of force targeted civilian causing collateral damages and local resentment. A principal of a Public High School in Shin Warsak reflected on the devastation of the school: "Seven rooms completely destroyed. Three other rooms were partially damaged, doors and windows had been shot open with bullets, and documents were littered all over the place. It appeared that our soldiers had conquered my school."[65] A local tribesman explained the desperation of the tribesmen over the excessive and indiscriminate use of force by the military forces: "Tribal people are angry. Their houses and villages are being attacked. They have no option but to fight back."[66] In addition, during operations, the military resorted to despotic methods involving arbitrary arrests, unfair detentions, economic blockades, and the destruction of property. Hasan Abbas termed the Pakistan army's brutal way of dealing with the tribes in the FATA as reminiscent of the means employed by the army in 1971 in East Pakistan, which later seceded from Pakistan and established an independent country named Bangladesh.[67]

The local people of the FATA affirmed that military operations caused a lot of collateral damage and killed many innocent tribesmen.[68] During a military operation at the beginning of 2008 in South Waziristan, over 4,000 houses owned by local people were demolished. In addition, more than 60 government school buildings, healthcare centres, telecommunication facilities, and electricity and other infrastructure were also destroyed.[69] Similarly in an operation in Bajaur, over 2,000 houses were destroyed and scores of civilian causalities occurred.[70] Pakistan's military operations inflicted heavy human and economic losses on the local tribesmen and created strong feelings of alienation.[71]

The use of conventional force caused serious damage to the lives and property of the local tribesmen that translated into local sympathy for insurgents. Marvin Weinbaum noted that "Heavy-handed military operations always threaten to create additional recruits to militant groups and evoke public sympathy."[72] Bombardment of the tribal people by long-range artillery guns and Cobra helicopter gunships further enraged them and facilitated recruitment by the rebel leaders. Shah explained that "indiscriminate use of force caused numerous civilian casualties", that aroused the local tribes' ire and pushed them towards the rebels for protection.[73] A former federal law minister described the military's despotic methods as responsible for fuelling insurgency. He said, "There is seething anger amongst the locals which might well be fuelling support for the militants amongst even those who were otherwise indifferent and whose support could have been critical to the success of the anti-terrorist campaign."[74]

These atrocities by the forces were successfully exploited by the insurgent leaders to mobilise local support and create disdain towards the army. A key leader of TTP once said, "If the goal of the Pakistani Army is to make a helpless people cry, make orphans cry, force the displacement of the population, orphan children, martyr old and young men, humiliate the people, and bomb madaris and mosques, then it has achieved its target."[75] In addition, many young tribesmen joined the insurgents' ranks, predominantly to exact retribution for the deaths of family members killed during the indiscriminate bombing of by the army, and despite not approving of the insurgents' ideology.[76] An observer of the FATA insurgency, Aqil Shah, explained that Pakistani army's conventional way of fighting insurgency helped the insurgents' cause. He said, "Its [Pakistani military] heavy use of artillery and helicopter gunships failed to 'flush out' militants or deny them sanctuary. Instead, the indiscriminate use of force caused numerous civilian casualties, angering locals and thus helping the insurgents."[77]

Similarly, the US forces' use of Unmanned Ariel Vehicles (UAVs) to shoot Hellfire missiles at targets inside the FATA is also believed to have caused significant collateral damage including the death of innocent women and children. This created severe resentment and inflamed anti-US and anti-Pakistan feelings.[78] According to the New America Foundation, between 2004 and 2010, 158 UAV attacks were carried out, causing between 311 to 530 civilian deaths. Other sources reported over 700 civilian deaths in these attacks in 2009 alone.[79] The attacks were also considered an important factor in motivating the locals to join the insurgents' camps in the FATA. This can be best understood through a statement given by Baitullah Mehsud, the most ferocious leader of the TTP, who said, "I spent three months trying to recruit and got only 10–15 persons. One United States attack, and I got 150 volunteers."[80]

Weak Police Forces

Apart from the military and paramilitary forces, the role of local security forces is believed to be an important factor in deterring or fighting insurgency.[81] A counterinsurgency campaign appears weak when local security forces, such as the police, are incompetent and ill-equipped. In addition, the use of military forces is not always possible because of the frequent mobility of insurgent forces. In contrast to the military forces, the police are permanently stationed locally, enabling them to have a better understanding of the threat environment and better local intelligence.[82]

Counterinsurgency efforts are often ineffective if the local security forces fail to provide security for local people against the predations of the insurgents. The pursuit of personal safety by the local population appears to be an influential factor in determining their support for either insurgents or counterinsurgents.[83] Inability of the local security forces to provide security to the local population forces the latter to acquiesce to insurgents' rule.[84] In addition, local people tend to support the insurgents to avoid any harm by them. Accordingly, support of the local population is a precondition for the defeat of an insurgency.[85]

Weak police forces in the FATA were simply incapable of providing security to the local people or fighting the insurgents. As discussed earlier, the Pakistani government had traditionally had weak control of the FATA region. The strength of the local security forces had for a long time been minimal because the tribes themselves were responsible for the security of the tribal territory. In addition, the local security forces had inept training and lacked modern and sophisticated weapons. These local forces proved inefficient and ineffective when the insurgents started challenging the writ of the state. Moreover, the local forces were not capable of providing security to the local people. Many people who were not initially aligned with the insurgents began to be.

The police in the FATA broadly consisted of three forces: the paramilitary Frontier Corps (FC), the dominant actor in law enforcement; tribal levies (official tribal militias); and khassadars (tribal police). In addition, the

Frontier Constabulary, an armed police force, also operated in an area bordering the FATA and the settled districts. These security forces had poor training and lacked modern weaponry. For example, the Frontier Corps was described as poorly "equipped and badly trained".[86] An American scholar, Christine Fair, affirmed that the FC was "inadequately trained and equipped and has been ill-prepared" to protect the indigenous people.[87] Similarly, the levies were supplied with small arms and little ammunition, whereas khassadars used their own weapons.[88] They were also underpaid. For example, levies were paid a monthly salary of Rs. 3,500 (roughly US$43).[89] It is not surprising that these inadequately equipped, poorly trained and underpaid security forces were unable to maintain law and order and provide protection to the local population. It was only after July 2009 that the government paid attention and began to enhance the strength and the professional capacity of khassadars and levies to prepare them to control areas after the military operations had cleared them of insurgents. Both forces were promised better salaries and improved equipment and training.[90]

The growing power of the insurgents and the inability of local forces to act against them created an environment of fear and insecurity in the FATA. This was particularly the case in North and South Waziristan and Bajaur, where the militants had a strong presence. Fear of the local militants contributed significantly to local acceptance of the insurgents' rule.[91] Furthermore, the local militants killed many *maliks* and tribal elders who opposed their rule or cooperated with the government. The Interior Minister, Aftab Sherpao, reported to the cabinet that, as of April 2006, the Taliban had killed 150 pro-government *maliks* in both Waziristan agencies.[92] These occurrences further weakened the existing administrative system and enhanced the status of the local militants in the area.

Instead of accepting that it was a government failure for not providing security to the tribal elders and *maliks*, the army officials maintained that the *maliks'* assassinations had resulted from tribal rivalries, and not because the state had co-opted these *maliks*. [93] The government's irresponsible attitude towards the security of the local population further annoyed the tribesmen. In addition, it provided ample opportunity to the insurgents to gain influence over the local population. Ahmed Rashid discussed the military's failure to provide protection to the local people and the ultimate control of the insurgents, noting that:

> FATA is now almost entirely controlled by the Pakistani Taliban militias [FATA insurgents].... The last few years the Army has failed to protect tribal elders, civil society professionals like teachers and doctors, and local people who were all opposed to the Taliban. As a result these people have either been killed by the Taliban or they have fled.... The result is that the Pakistani Taliban is in total control.[94]

Unchecked by the local security forces, the local militants established parallel administrations in some of the FATA agencies. They organised committees to collect funds, impose taxes on businesses and enforced punishments on local offenders. A well-informed resident of North Waziristan observed, "The [Pakistani] Taliban have established summary trial courts and police the area under their control."[95] A local journalist observed that the insurgents were recruiting, training, and raising money with impunity.[96] Fair explained the rise of the insurgents and their growing control over the local population, maintaining that:

> local militants gradually became a parallel government in the tribal areas... . The traditional *jirga* was formally banned. In its place, aggrieved parties had to seek intervention from the Taliban representative in their village, who performed the functions of police officer, administrator, and judge. Local militants ... banned music stores, videos, and televisions and issued edicts that men had to grow beards. They also continued to target pro-government tribal elders, forcing many to flee.[97]

The local militants often boasted about their growing power. They claimed that "The Taliban [insurgents] in Waziristan are capturing hearts and minds. We see the tribes who were struggling for tens of years accepting arbitration by Taliban [insurgents]."[98]

Government's Negotiations with Insurgents from the Position of Weakness

Negotiations with insurgents without destroying their power may allow an insurgency to grow and get stronger. Most importantly, negotiations with insurgents from a position of government weakness is likely to be interpreted by insurgents as a sign of weakness that may embolden them. The Pakistani government adopted the strategy of negotiations with the insurgents for several reasons. Historically, counterinsurgency campaigns have mostly proven to be more costly, protracted, and difficult than estimated at the planning stage.[99] This may have driven the Pakistani government to choose to pursue negotiations. Moreover, conducting military operations in the tribal areas was quite challenging due to the ideological and physical proximity with Afghanistan, as well as "entrenched kinship, tribal bonds, and hostile terrain."[100] In addition, the Pakistani officials had underestimated the growing threat of insurgency in the FATA.[101] Massive military losses due to inept and ineffective military operations, described elsewhere, also led the government to initiate negotiations with the insurgents. An eminent local journalist, Safdar Dawar, maintained that most of the military operations were hasty and short-lived, and the larger military campaigns remained mostly inconclusive and ended with the signing of peace agreements.[102] Therefore, the Pakistani government negotiated peace agreements from a position of weakness, which allowed the militants to extract significant concessions from the state without offering anything in return.[103]

The military brokered peace agreements with the tribal militants in South Waziristan in 2004 and 2005, and in North Waziristan in 2006. After the peace agreements, the government stopped military operations, freed captured militants, and announced an amnesty for foreign militants, predicated on conditions such as their registration with the government and the surrendering of weapons. In return, the tribal militants made commitments to the government to renounce violence and refrain from attacking the Pakistani military, as well as cross-border attacks in Afghanistan. However, the tribal militants did not maintain their pledges and soon resumed insurgent activities. The peace agreements served only to enhance the insurgents' control over the territory in exchange for fake promises to stop attacking the government's installations and troops. An eminent scholar, Marvin Weinbaum, contended that "No means were provided to enforce deals, and the Pakistani government accepted at face-value pledges by militants."[104] In addition, Pakistan's negotiating approach had a fundamental problem: "All the agreements [with insurgents] were reached from a position of government weakness rather than strength."[105] Aqil Shah explained how the Pakistani military strategy of making peace agreements provided the militants with the necessary time to strengthen themselves:

> By giving amnesty to militants and capitulating to their demands, these accords clearly emboldened them to create Taliban-style administrative and judicial structures in the tribal agencies, from which they are now busy spreading their influence into other tribal agencies and the rest of the NWFP.[106]

Discussion of the various peace agreements between the government and the insurgents follows.

Shakai Peace Agreement – 2004 (South Waziristan Agency)

After a failed military operation that caused huge losses, the military signed the first peace agreement with the local militant leader, Nek Muhammad, on 24 April 2004.[107] During the negotiations, Nek Muhammad put several demands before the government such as the withdrawal of military forces from South Waziristan, compensation for the losses suffered by local people and the release of 163 tribesmen arrested during the military operations.[108] Almost all demands were accepted by the government. In addition, the deal-making ceremony was held at a madrassa near Wana, a place chosen by the tribal militants, which showed the militants had the upper hand.[109] Furthermore, the militant leader, Nek Muhammad, negotiated the deal from a position of strength because he had emerged victorious in his fight with the military. An expert on the FATA attested this, "Pakistan's army was in a weak situation on the ground, and it was an inappropriate time to opt for a negotiated deal."[110]

The ensuing agreement further weakened the government's writ. The agreement did not use the term 'surrender' and it read as "reconciliation between estranged brothers."[111] This reconciliation was construed by the tribal people as the "army's tacit acceptance of their opponents as equally powerful and legitimate."[112] Nek Muhammad "pledged his allegiance to a state that barely ruled the FATA anyway."[113] The militants did not surrender weapons, which were rather 'offered' to the military as a ceremonial gesture. This was taken by the local people as surrender by the army, rather than by the tribal militants. Nek Mohammad boasted later that "I did not go to them, they came to my place. That should make it clear who surrendered to whom."[114]

As a result, the agreement played a role in the escalation of the insurgency. The tribal militants achieved legitimacy and a higher standing than the traditional tribal leaders in the eyes of the local population. A scholar, Hassan Abbas, contended, "Pakistan's government had accorded them an elevated status by engaging them in negotiations directly."[115] The tribal militants felt emboldened after the peace agreement and continued to provide shelter to the foreign militants and to assist them in attacking the coalition forces in Afghanistan. The government maintained that the tribesmen had pledged to hand over foreign militants, while the militants denied making any such commitment. Nek Muhammad reiterated his pledge to continue to fight against US-led coalition forces in Afghanistan.[116] He laid the foundation for defiance against the state by becoming a role model for young radicals of the area. In June 2004, he was killed by a US missile strike near Wana.[117] However, the insurgency continued to grow in the coming years as the release of the militants stipulated in the deal proved lethal, accelerating the pace of insurgency and intensity of violence. President Musharaf, reflecting on the motivation for making a peace deal with the militants and its failure, said in an interview in 2006:

> I think that it did not prove good. But one must not speak with hindsight. You have to apply all instruments. We thought if we reached an agreement that would be the end of it. No, it proved wrong, because the people who got involved on the other side, they double-crossed.[118]

The Pakistani military alleged the militants violated the agreement and resorted to the use of force against them. However, the government appeared weak in this whole episode.

Sararogha Peace Deal – 2005 (South Waziristan)

Military operations in the Mehsud-inhabited areas of South Waziristan also resulted in huge losses for the military. This ultimately led the military to engage the tribal militants in peace negotiations. A peace settlement was finally negotiated and signed with Baitullah Mehsud, the tribal militants' leader on 7 February 2005 at Sararogha, South Waziristan.[119] Like the Shakai peace deal, this was an unwritten agreement and lacked any enforcement mechanism. Noticeably, in this agreement the government did not demand that local militants surrender foreign militants and there was no mention of carrying out cross-border attacks in Afghanistan. Financial payments were also made to the local militants, but some claimed that these payments were offered to compensate for property damages in South Waziristan resulting from the military operations.[120]

This agreement further strengthened the militants' resolve, allowing them to expand their influence. Baitullah continued to provide shelter to the foreign militants and publicly expressed his determination to continue with the jihad against the US-led coalition in Afghanistan.[121] In a press briefing, Baitullah said that the Pakistani military was forced to make the peace agreement, adding that "Pakistan has also realised that fighting tribal people is weakening its ability. ... This agreement will last unless the government violates it."[122]

Baitullah effectively used this time to mobilise more people to join him. He was successful in raising a force of almost 20,000 militants by the end of 2007.[123] Mahmood Shah, the former secretary of the FATA contended, "The government policy of appeasement gave Mehsud a free hand to recruit and motivate."[124] Moreover, Baitullah-linked militants killed those tribal elders who were considered sympathetic to the government.[125] Baitullah also increasingly coordinated with other tribal militant groups who were engaged in resisting the government in other parts of the FATA. Finally, Baitullah unilaterally abrogated the agreement with the government and laid down the foundation for Tehrik-e-Taliban Pakistan (TTP) in December 2007.

Peace Deal in North Waziristan – 2006

Like the previous two peace agreements, the agreement signed in North Waziristan in 2006 was motivated by the failure of the military approach that could not subdue the insurgents. Newly appointed governor, Ali Jan Orakzia, a native Pashtun of the FATA and former XI Corps Commander Peshawar, announced his strategy as being "Three-pronged with a political process and dialogue in the lead, followed by socio-economic development, and military action wherever required."[126] By signing a peace agreement with the tribal militants in North Waziristan on 5 September 2006, Orakzia attempted to restore the *status quo* in the FATA as it was before 2002.[127] In the previous two peace deals, the political administration and the tribal elders were marginalised, and the military was at the forefront in making the peace agreements with local militants. This time, the government involved the political administration as well as the tribal elders in the negotiations process with the militants. However, this peace deal was in tatters after a brief period of only ten months of its signing.[128]

This peace deal is also believed to have strengthened the local militants. The previous two peace agreements had failed to deliver the desired objectives; instead, they had emboldened the militants operating in other parts of the FATA. Regarding this peace arrangement, an expert asserted that "Whoever challenges the government's writ derives more leverage during negotiations."[129] Hoisting the militants' flag (al-Rayah) at the stadium where the agreement was signed was a practical manifestation of the growing power and confidence of the militants and represented a mockery of the supremacy of government authority in the area. An editorial in a leading English-language newspaper contended, "[T]he government has all but caved in to the demands of the militants. More ominously, the agreement seems to be a tacit acknowledgment by the government of the growing power and authority of the local Taliban."[130] After a brief period, the militants resumed their anti-state activities and supported cross-border attacks in Afghanistan. NATO officials believed that there was a remarkable increase in the attacks inside Afghanistan after this agreement.[131] A Defence Intelligence Assessment (DIA) noted that:

> Pakistan's border with Afghanistan remains a haven for Al Qaida's leadership and other extremists. In a September [2006] accord with the Pakistan government, North Waziristan tribes agreed to curtail attacks into Afghanistan, cease attacks on Pakistani forces and expel foreign fighters. However, the tribes have not abided by most terms of the agreement.[132]

All the three peace agreements failed to deliver that further weakened the writ of the state. These deals in fact provided "much-needed respite to the militants, enabling them to re-group and re-organise themselves."[133] The peace deals with the tribal militants undoubtedly increased the power of the insurgents in the tribal areas. A Pakistani Ministry of Interior report marked the government's policy as "Appeasement towards the Taliban, which has further emboldened them."[134] The report further cautioned about a possible expansion of the insurgency from the tribal areas to the settled areas: "Talibanisation [of the insurgency] has not only unfolded potential threats to our security, but is also casting its dark shadows over FATA and now in the settled areas adjoining the tribal belt. The reality is that it is spreading."[135]

An ad-hoc approach coupled with a lack of political will and shortterm gains guided the negotiations strategy pursued by the Pakistani government that ultimately served to strengthen the FATA insurgency. The various peace deals were "geared initially toward reducing losses for the military, which was not accustomed to the terrain, lacked weapons needed in the area, and initially was insufficiently motivated to take on militants."[136] In addition, these peace agreements basically aimed at containing the insurgency, not eliminating it. An expert maintained, "Apparently, the purpose of these deals was to limit the conflict zone from expanding and avoid a head-on collision with the militants. These objectives were far from being achieved, and in fact these 'deals' proved to be counterproductive."[137] As a result of these peace deals, local people were left at the mercy of the local militants. Brigadier Asad Munir (a retired ISI official) acknowledged that:

> A focused strategy to deal with terrorists was never followed. In September 2006, the government concluded another peace deal with the Taliban of North Waziristan. Because of this deal, foreign militants started operating openly. The only option for the locals was to accept Taliban rule.[138]

Furthermore, by engaging the armed groups in peace negotiations, the Pakistani state provided them with the much-needed legitimacy and marginalised the traditional power elites such as *maliks* and tribal elders. According to an analyst, Samir Puri:

> Bargain with or entering into agreement with an armed group would run the risk of legitimising them and influencing power structures within the armed group in ways that could not be anticipated, such as inadvertently boosting (or perhaps eroding) the standing of those individuals that the state engaged with over those that it did not.[139]

Conclusion

This chapter demonstrates that the Pakistani state poor counterinsurgency strategy was mainly responsible for the growth of the Taliban insurgency in the FATA. The Pakistani government lacked the necessary political will to take the insurgency seriously which led to a weak response from the government. Lacking counterinsurgency skills, the Pakistani forces were largely conventional in terms of their training and equipment. Moreover, the military forces did not develop a counterinsurgency doctrine and largely kept their conventional capabilities intact. This was primarily because of their perennial focus on enmity with India. The use of conventional forces to fight insurgency proved counterproductive. The indiscriminate use of force caused civilian damages and human rights abuses that facilitated the success of insurgent recruitment from the local population, thereby swelling their numbers. In addition, inadequate and poorly skilled local security forces were unable to offer protection to the local population against the insurgents which forced the local communities to compromise with the insurgents' rule. Seeking a political solution is generally considered to be a valuable part of a counterinsurgency strategy. However, the Pakistani government's approach of negotiating and signing peace agreements with the insurgents faced a fundamental problem in that the negotiations were invariably conducted without defeating the insurgents completely. These negotiations from a position of weakness boosted the insurgents' confidence in their ability and power and exposed their opponent's vulnerabilities. These poor counterinsurgency tactics practiced by the Pakistani military proved instrumental in escalating the FATA insurgency, making it a powerful movement. The next chapter demonstrates that an improved counterinsurgency strategy by the Pakistani government after 2009 led to the gradual decline of the insurgency.

Notes

1 See the editorial "60 Miles from Islamabad," *New York Times*, April 26, 2009.
2 Paul Richter and Christi Parsons, "Obama Prepares to Meet with Leaders of Afghanistan, Pakistan," *Los Angeles Times*, May 5, 2009.
3 According to army spokesman Major General Athar Abbas, "about 200 militants charged the fort from four sides … they broke through the fort's wall with rockets," "Militants Overrun Pakistan Fort," *BBC News*, 2008, http://news.bbc.co.uk/2/hi/south_asia/7191200.stm.
4 Syed Manzar Abbas Zaidi, "The United States and the Counterinsurgency: The Peace Process in Pakistan," *American Foreign Policy Interests* 31, no. 3 (May 18, 2009): 149–65; Mukhtar A. Khan, "A Profile of Militant Groups in Bajaur Tribal Agency," *Terrorism Monitor* (2009)
5 Carlotta Gall and Ismail Khan, "In Pakistan, Doubts Over the Fight in Tribal Area," *New York Times*, February 12, 2008.
6 Gall and Khan, "In Pakistan, Doubts Over the Fight in Tribal Area," *New York Times*, February 12, 2008.
7 Mushtaq Yusufzai, "Taliban Warns of Attack on Capital," *The News*, June 10, 2008.
8 Anatol Lieven, "Counter-Insurgency in Pakistan: The Role of Legitimacy," *Small Wars & Insurgencies* 28, no. 1 (2017): 170–72.
9 Pervez Musharaf, *In the Line of Fire: A Memoir* (New York: Simon and Schuster, 2006), 202.
10 Shaukat Qadir, "The State's Responses to the Pakistani Taliban Onslaught," in *Insurgency and Counterinsurgency in South Asia through a Peacebuilding Lens*, ed. Moeed Yusuf (Washington, DC: United States Institute of Peace, 2014), 132.
11 Haider Ali Hussein Mullick, *Helping Pakistan Defeat the Taliban: A Joint Action Agenda for the United States and Pakistan* (Clinton Township, MI: Institute for Social Policy and Understanding, 2009), 17.
12 Clay Ramsay, Steven Kull, Stephen Weber, and Evan Lewis, "Pakistani Public Opinion on the Swat Conflict, Afghanistan, and the US," *WorldPublicOpinion.org* (July 2008): 16–24.
13 C. Christine Fair and Seth G. Jones, *Counterinsurgency in Pakistan* (Santa Monica, CA: Rand Corporation, 2010), 37.
14 David J. Kilcullen, "Terrain, Tribes, and Terrorist: Pakistan, 2006–2008," *Brookings Counterinsurgency and Pakistan Paper Series*, No. 3, 2009.
15 M. L. R. Smith, "A Tradition That Never Was: Critiquing the Critique of British COIN," *Small Wars Journal* (2012).
16 Paul Dixon, "'Hearts and Minds'? British Counter-Insurgency from Malay to Iraq," *Journal of Strategic Studies* 32, no. 3 (2009): 357.
17 David Galula, *Counterinsurgency Warfare: Theory and Practice* (Westport, CT: Praeger Security International, 2006 [1964]), 55.
18 Dixon, "'Hearts and Minds'? British Counter-Insurgency," 358.
19 Shamshad Ahmad, "Post 9/11 Foreign Policy of Pakistan," *Criterion Quarterly* 1, no. 1 (2006): 3.
20 Bruce Riedel, "Pakistan: The Critical Battlefield," Current History 107, no. 712 (2008): 358.
21 "President Musharaf Address to the Nation," *The News*, March 8, 2002.

22 Musharaf, *In the Line of Fire: A Memoir*, 202.
23 "U.S. Department of State, Congressional Budget Justification for Foreign Operations, Fiscal Year 2007," 2007, http://www.state.gov/documents/organiza tion/60641.pdf.
24 Hari Sud, "Pakistan: Why Is Mushrraf Smiling These Days?," *South Asia Analysis Group, Paper No. 1188* (2004).
25 "Pakistan Gets $256 Million for Support US," *Daily Times*, August 1, 2003.
26 Craig Cohen and Derek Chollet, "When $10 Billion Is Not Enough: Rethinking U.S. Strategy toward Pakistan," *The Washington Quarterly* 30, no. 2 (2007): 13.
27 K. Alan Kronstadt, *Pakistan–U.S. Relations*, (US: Congress Research Service Report, 2006), 8.
28 Ahmed Rashid, "Pakistan's Worrisome Pullback," *The Washington Post*, June 6, 2008.
29 Fair and Jones, *Counterinsurgency in Pakistan*, 83.
30 Fair and Jones, *Counterinsurgency in Pakistan*, 83.
31 Mark Mazetti and Eric Schmitt, "CIA Outlines Pakistan's Links with Militants," *New York Times*, July 30, 2008.
32 Aqil Shah, "Pakistan After Musharraf: Praetorianism and Terrorism," *Journal of Democracy* 19, no. 4 (2008): 22.
33 Former DG Inter-Services Public Relations, Maj. General retired, Athar Abbas (Rawalpindi), interview by author, 5 April, 2014.
34 Ayaz Wazir, a former ambassador and resident of South Waziristan (Peshawar), interview by author, 4 November, 2013.
35 Shah, "Pakistan After Musharraf," 17.
36 Interview with a graduate student, Bajaur Agency, FATA. Cited in Amnesty International, *As If Hell Fell on Me: The Human Rights Crisis in Northwest Pakistan* (London: Amnesty Internatioinal, 2010), 53.
37 Syed Manzar Abbas Zaidi, "Pakistan's Anti-Taliban Counter-Insurgency," *The RUSI Journal* 155, no. 1 (February 2010): 13.
38 Fair and Jones, *Counterinsurgency in Pakistan*, 54.
39 Marvin G Weinbaum, "Hard Choices in Countering Insurgency and Terrorism along Pakistan's North-West Frontier," *Journal of International Affairs* 63, no. 1 (2009): 75.
40 Weinbaum, "Hard Choices in Countering Insurgency," 76.
41 Cited in International Crisis Group, *Pakistan's Tribal Areas: Appeasing the Militants* (ICG: Brussels, 2006), 15.
42 Kitson, *Low Intensity Operations: Subversion, Insurgency, and Peacekeeping*, 200.
43 Roger Trinuier, *Modern Warfare: A French View of Counterinsurgency, Trans. Daniel Lee* (New York: Praeger, 1964), 3.
44 Nagl, *Learning to Eat Soap with a Knife: Counterinsurgency Lessons from Malaya and Vietnam*, xxii.
45 C. Christine Fair and Seth G. Jones, *Counterinsurgency in Pakistan*, 37.
46 Aqil Shah, "Pakistan After Musharraf," 22.
47 Weinbaum, "Hard Choices in Countering Insurgency," 77.
48 Rashid, "Pakistan's Worrisome Pullback."
49 Sameer Lalwani, "Pakistan's COIN Flip: The Recent History of Pakistani Military Counterinsurgency Operations in the NWFP and FATA," *Counterterrorism Strategy Initiative Policy Paper*, April 2010, 1.
50 See Michael D. Maples, "Annual Threat Assessment: Statement Before the Committee on Armed Services United States Senate" (February 2008), 22; Michael D. Maples, "Annual Threat Assessment: Statement Before the Committee on Armed Services, United States Senate" (March 2009), 12.
51 Weinbaum, "Hard Choices in Countering Insurgency," 77.

52   Maples, "Annual Threat Assessment," 22; Maples, "Annual Threat Assessment," 12.
53   Samarjit Ghosh, "Insurgency in the FATA & NWFP: Challenges & Prospects for the Pakistan Army," *Manekshaw Paper, No. 6, Centre for Land Warfare Studies* (2008): 16.
54   Anthony H. Cordesman and Varun Vira, *Pakistan – Violence versus Stability: A National Net Assessment* (Washington, DC: Centre for Strategic and International Studies, 2011), 76.
55   "Pakistan and the Taliban: A Real Offensive or a Phony War?," *The Economist*, April 30, 2009.
56   Ghosh, "Insurgency in the FATA & NWFP," 18.
57   Frank Kitson, *Low Intensity Operations: Subversion, Insurgency, and Peacekeeping* (London: Faber and Faber, 1971), 84–85, 87.
58   Jeremy M. Weinstein, *Inside Rebellion: The Politics of Insurgent Violence* (Cambridge: Cambridge University Press, 2007), 37.
59   Zaidi, "Pakistan's Anti-Taliban Counter-Insurgency," 15.
60   Constantin Melnik quoted in Austin Long, *On "Other War": Lessons from Five Decades of RAND Counterinsurgency Research* (Santa Monica, CA: RAND Corporation, 2006), 27.
61   Zaidi, "Pakistan's Anti-Taliban Counter-Insurgency."
62   Shah, "Pakistan After Musharraf," 22.
63   Zaidi, "Pakistan's Anti-Taliban Counter-Insurgency," 15.
64   David Kilcullen, *The Accidental Guerrilla: Fighting Small Wars in the Midst of a Big One* (London: Hurst, 2009), 237.
65   Rahimullah Yusufzai and Sailab Mahsud, "Troops Pull out of Azam Warsak Area," *The News*, March 29, 2004.
66   Ismail Khan, "Govt Announces Ceasefire: Jirga to Negotiate Militants' Surrender," *Dawn*, March 22, 2004.
67   Hassan Abbas, *Pakistan's Troubled Frontier* (Washington, DC: Jamestown Foundation, 2009), 164, 235.
68   Zaidi, "Pakistan's Anti-Taliban Counter-Insurgency," 10.
69   "Over 4,000 Houses Destroyed in Waziristan Operation: Report," *Dawn*, November 8, 2008.
70   Anwarullah Khan, "Four-Day Truce Sparks Jubilation in Bajaur," *Dawn*, February 25, 2009.
71   International Crisis Group, *Pakistan: Countering Militancy in FATA* (ICG: Brussels, 2009), 1.
72   Weinbaum, "Hard Choices in Countering Insurgency," 78.
73   Shah, "Pakistan After Musharraf," 22.
74   International Crisis Group, *Pakistan's Tribal Areas: Appeasing the Militants*, 15.
75   Shehzad H. Qazi, "Rebels of the Frontier: Origins, Organization, and Recruitment of the Pakistani Taliban," *Small Wars & Insurgencies* 22, no. 4 (2011): 595.
76   Qazi, "Rebels of the Frontier," 595.
77   Shah, "Pakistan After Musharraf," 22.
78   Shuja Nawaz, *FATA – A Most Dangerous Place: Meeting the Challenge of Militancy and Terror in the Federally Administered Tribal Areas of Pakistan* (Washington DC: Center for Strategic & International Studies, 2009), 15.
79   Qazi, "Rebels of the Frontier," 595.
80   Nawaz, *FATA – A Most Dangerous Place*, 18.
81   Fair and Jones, *Counterinsurgency in Afghanistan*, 10.
82   Fair and Jones, *Counterinsurgency in Afghanistan*, 16.
83   Galula, *Counterinsurgency Warfare: Theory and Practice*, 8, 16, 54.

84 Cited in Alexander Grenoble and William Rose, "David Galula's Counter-insurgency: Occam's Razor and Colombia," *Civil Wars* 13, no. 3 (2011): 284.

85 Galula, *Counterinsurgency Warfare: Theory and Practice,* 8, 16, 54.

86 Rashid, "Pakistan's Worrisome Pullback."

87 C. Christine Fair, "U.S.–Pakistan Relations: Assassination, Instability, and the Future of U.S. Policy, Testimony before the House Foreign Affairs Committee, Subcommittee on the Middle East and South Asia," January 16, 2008.

88 International Crisis Group, "Pakistan: Countering Militancy in FATA," 17.

89 Khalid Kheshgi, "5,000 More Levies Personnel Being Re- Cruited to Man Cleared Areas," *Daily Times,* July 31, 2009.

90 Kheshgi, "5,000 More Levies Personnel Being Ibid."

91 A journalist from North Waziristan, Safdar Dawar (Peshawar), interview by author, January 22, 2014.

92 "Editorial: Admitting Taliban Rule in FATA," *Daily Times,* April 19, 2006.

93 "80 Foreign Terrorists in North Waziristan," *Daily Times,* July 25, 2005.

94 Scott Horton, "Inside the Pakistan-Taliban Relationship: Six Questions for Ahmed Rashid, Author of Descent into Chaos," *Harper's Magazine,* July 30, 2008, http://harpers.org/archive/2008/07/hbc-90003347.

95 International Crisis Group, "Pakistan's Tribal Areas: Appeasing the Militants," 23.

96 A journalist from North Waziristan, Safdar Dawar (Peshawar), interview by author, January 22, 2014.

97 Fair and Jones, *Counterinsurgency in Pakistan,* 55.

98 Fair and Jones, *Counterinsurgency in Pakistan,* 56.

99 Sarah Sewall, *The U.S. Army/Marine Corps Counterinsurgency Field Manual* (Chicago, IL: University of Chicago Press, 2007), 3.

100 Zaidi, "Pakistan's Anti-Taliban Counter-Insurgency," 13.

101 Hassan Abbas, "Militancy in Pakistan's Borderland: Implications for the Nation and for Afghan Policy," *Century Foundation Report* (2010), 23.

102 A journalist from North Waziristan, Safdar Dawar (Peshawar), interview by author, 22 January, 2014.

103 Wali Aslam, "Whose Interest? Whose Peace? An Evaluation of Pakistan's Peace Agreements with the Taliban in the Tribal Areas (2004–2015)," *Studies in Conflict & Terrorism* (2020).

104 Weinbaum, "Hard Choices in Countering Insurgency," 76.

105 After the 2006 agreement in North Waziristan, infiltration into southeastern Afghanistan increased three fold. Saleem Shahzad, "The Knife at Pakistan's Throat," *Asia Times,* September 2, 2006.

106 Shah, "Pakistan After Musharraf," 23.

107 Shabana Fayyaz, "Towards a Durable Peace in Waziristan," *Pakistan Security Research Unit,* Brief No. 10, 2007.

108 C. Christine Fair and Seth G. Jones, "Pakistan's War Within," *Survival* 51, no. 6 (December 2009–January 2010): 170–171.

109 Owais Tohid, "The New Frontier," *Newsline* (Pakistan), April 2004; Ismail Khan, "Five Militants Pardoned for Peaceful Life: Aliens Asked to Surrender by 30th," *Dawn,* April 25, 2004.

110 Abbas, "Militancy in Pakistan's Borderland, " 15.

111 Rahimullah Yusufzai, "All Quiet on the North Western Front," *Newsline, Pakistan,* May 2004.

112 Fair and Jones, "Pakistan's War Within," 171.

113 Samir Puri, *Pakistan's War on Terrorism: Strategies for Combating Jihadist Armed Groups Since 9/11* (New York: Routledge, 2012), 56.

114 Iqbal Khattak, "I Did Not Surrender to the Military, Said Nek Mohammad," *Friday Times,* 2004.

115   Iqbal Khattak, "I Did Not Surrender to the Military," 17.
116   A local resident of South Waziristan (Peshawar), interview by author, February 5, 2014.
117   Ismail Khan and Dilawar Khan Wazir, "Night Raid Kills Nek, Four Other Militants," *Dawn*, June 19, 2004.
118   "President Musharaf Interview on PBS Documentary 'Frontline: The Return of the Taliban,'" October 3, 2006, www.pbs.org/wgbh/pages/frontline/taliban.
119   Shamim Shahid, "Baitullah, Supporters Lay Down Arms," *The Nation*, February 9, 2005.
120   "Pakistan Pays Tribe Al Qaeda Debt," *BBC News*, February 9, 2005.
121   For Baitullah Mehsud's statement, see Haroon Rashid, "Pakistan Taleban Vow More Violence," *BBC News*, January 29, 2007.
122   "Baitullah and 35 Other Get Government Amnesty," *Daily Times*, February 8, 2005.
123   "Spotlight Falls on Taliban Man Accused of Murdering Benazir," *Daily Times*, January 28, 2008.
124   "Spotlight Falls on Taliban."
125   "Spotlight Falls on Taliban."
126   Lieutenant General (Retired) Ali Jan Orakzia told after relinquishing the post. Cited in Puri, *Pakistan's War on Terrorism*, 60.
127   Lt. Gen. Ali Jan Orakzai, former Corps Commander Peshawar and Governor Khyber Pakhtunkhwa (Rawalpindi), interview by author, 5 April, 2014.
128   "Soldier Killed in Pakistan Militant Attack," *Dawn*, July 26, 2007; Haji Mujtiba, "Militants Threaten Attacks in Pakistan's Waziristan," *Reuters*, July 17, 2007; "North Waziristan Clerics to Launch 'Silent Protest'," *Daily Times*, August 3, 2007.
129   Abbas, "Militancy in Pakistan's Borderland," 20.
130   "Back to Square One?" Editorial, *The News*, September 7, 2006.
131   "Taliban Attacks Double After Pakistan's Deal with Militants," *Guardian*, September 29, 2006.
132   Michael D. Maples, "Current and Projected National Security Threats to the United States, Statement for the Record, Senate Select Committee on Intelligence Committee" (January 2007), 12.
133   Sayed G. B. Shah Bokhari, "How Peace Deals Help Only Militants," *The News*, July 31, 2008.
134   Ismail Khan, "Talibanisation Imperils Security, NSC Warned: Immediate Action Urged," *Dawn*, June 22, 2007.
135   Khan, "Talibanisation Imperils Security, NSC Warned."
136   Abbas, "Militancy in Pakistan's Borderland," 23.
137   Abbas, "Militancy in Pakistan's Borderland," 15.
138   Asad Munir, "How FATA Was Won by the Taliban," *Express Tribune*, June 21, 2010.
139   Puri, *Pakistan's War on Terrorism*, 65.

Bibliography

Abbas, Hassan. *Pakistan's Troubled Frontier*. Washington, DC: Jamestown Foundation, 2009.
Abbas, Hassan. "Militancy in Pakistan's Borderland: Implications for the Nation and for Afghan Policy. "*Century Foundation Report*, 2010.
Ahmad, Shamshad. "Post 9/11 Foreign Policy of Pakistan." *Criterion Quarterly* 1, no. 1 (2006): 1–34.

Amnesty International. *As If Hell Fell on Me: The Human Rights Crisis in Northwest Pakistan.* London: Amnesty International, 2010.

Aslam, Wali. "Whose Interest? Whose Peace? An Evaluation of Pakistan's Peace Agreements with the Taliban in the Tribal Areas (2004–2015)." *Studies in Conflict & Terrorism* (2020): 1–25.

"Back to Square One?," Editorial. *The News*, September 7, 2006.

"Baitullah and 35 Other Get Government Amnesty." *Daily Times*, February 8, 2005.

Bokhari, Sayed G. B. Shah. "How Peace Deals Help Only Militants." *The News*, July 31, 2008.

Cohen, Craig, and Derek Chollet, "When $10 Billion Is Not Enough: Rethinking U.S. Strategy toward Pakistan." *The Washington Quarterly* 30, no. 2 (2007): 7–19.

Cordesman, Anthony H., and Varun Vira. *Pakistan -Violence versus Stability: A National Net Assessment.* Washington, DC: Centre for Strategic and International Studies, 2011.

Dixon, Paul. "Hearts and Minds'? British Counter-Insurgency from Malay to Iraq." *Journal of Strategic Studies* 32, no. 3 (2009): 353–381.

"Editorial: Admitting Taliban Rule in FATA." *Daily Times*, April 19, 2006.

"80 Foreign Terrorists in North Waziristan." *Daily Times*, July 25, 2005.

Fair, Christine C. "U.S.–Pakistan Relations: Assassination, Instability, and the Future of U.S. Policy, testimony before the House Foreign Affairs Committee, Subcommittee on the Middle East and South Asia." January 16, 2008.

Fair, Christine C., and Seth G. Jones. "Pakistan's War Within." *Survival* 51, no. 6 (December2009–January 2010): 161–188.

Fair, Christine C., and Seth G. Jones. *Counterinsurgency in Pakistan.* Santa Monica, CA: Rand Corporation, 2010.

Fayyaz, Shabana. "Towards a Durable Peace in Waziristan." *Pakistan Security Research Unit*, Brief No. 10, 2007.

Gall, Carlotta, and Ismail Khan. "In Pakistan, Doubts Over the Fight in Tribal Area." *New York Times*, February 12, 2008.

Galula, David. *Counterinsurgency Warfare: Theory and Practice.* Westport, CT: Praeger Security International, 2006 [1964].

Ghosh, Samarjit. "Insurgency in the FATA & NWFP: Challenges & Prospects for the Pakistan Army." *Manekshaw Paper, No. 6*, Centre for Land Warfare Studies, 2008.

Grenoble, Alexander, and William Rose, "David Galula's Counterinsurgency: Occam's Razor and Colombia." *Civil Wars* 13, no. 3 (2011): 280–311.

Horton, Scott. "Inside the Pakistan-Taliban Relationship: Six Questions for Ahmed Rashid, Author of Descent into Chaos." *Harper's Magazine*, July 30, 2008. http://harpers.org/archive/2008/07/hbc-90003347.

International Crisis Group. *Pakistan's Tribal Areas: Appeasing the Militants.* Brussels: IGC, 2006.

International Crisis Group. *Pakistan: Countering Militancy in FATA.* Brussels: IGC, 2009.

Khan, Anwarullah. "Four-Day Truce Sparks Jubilation in Bajaur." *Dawn*, February 25, 2009.

Khan, Ismail. "Five Militants Pardoned for Peaceful Life: Aliens Asked to Surrender by 30th." *Dawn*, April 25, 2004.

Khan, Ismail. "Govt Announces Ceasefire: Jirga to Negotiate Militants' Surrender." *Dawn*, March 22, 2004.

Khan, Ismail. "Talibanisation Imperils Security, NSC Warned: Immediate Action Urged." *Dawn*, June 22, 2007.

Khan, Ismail, and Dilawar Khan Wazir, "Night Raid Kills Nek, Four Other Militants." *Dawn*, June 19, 2004.

Khan, Mukhtar A. "A Profile of Militant Groups in Bajaur Tribal Agency." *Terrorism Monitor* (2009).

Khattak, Iqbal. "I Did Not Surrender to the Military, Said Nek Mohammad," *Friday Times*, 2004.

Kheshgi, Khalid. "5,000 More Levies Personnel Being Re-Cruited to Man Cleared Areas." *Daily Times*, July 31, 2009.

Kilcullen, David J., "Terrain, Tribes, and Terrorist: Pakistan, 2006–2008". *Brookings Counterinsurgency and Pakistan Paper Series*, No. 3, 2009.

Kilcullen, David. *The Accidental Guerrilla: Fighting Small Wars in the Midst of a Big One* London: Hurst, 2009.

Kitson, Frank. *Low Intensity Operations: Subversion, Insurgency, and Peacekeeping.* London: Faber and Faber, 1971.

Kronstadt, K. Alan. *Pakistan–U.S. Relations.* US: Congress Research Service Report, 2006.

Lalwani, Sameer. "Pakistan's COIN Flip: The Recent History of Pakistani Military Counterinsurgency Operations in the NWFP and FATA." *Counterterrorism Strategy Initiative Policy Paper*, April2010.

Lieven, Anatol. "Counter-Insurgency in Pakistan: The Role of Legitimacy." *Small Wars & Insurgencies* 28, no. 1 (2017): 166–190.

Long, Austin. *On "Other War": Lessons from Five Decades of RAND Counterinsurgency Research.* Santa Monica, CA: RAND Corporation, 2006.

Maples, Michael D. "Current and Projected National Security Threats to the United States. Statement for the Record, Senate Select Committee on Intelligence Committee," January2007.

Maples, Michael D. "Annual Threat Assessment: Statement Before the Committee on Armed Services United States Senate." February2008.

Maples, Michael D. "Annual Threat Assessment: Statement Before the Committee on Armed Services, United States Senate." March2009.

Mazetti, Mark, and Eric Schmitt, "CIA Outlines Pakistan's Links with Militants." *New York Times*, July 30, 2008.

"Militants Overrun Pakistan Fort," *BBC News*, January 17, 2008. Accessed on December 17, 2019. http://news.bbc.co.uk/2/hi/south_asia/7191200.stm.

Mujtiba, Haji. "Militants Threaten Attacks in Pakistan's Waziristan." *Reuters*, July 17, 2007.

Mullick, Haider Ali Hussein. *Helping Pakistan Defeat the Taliban: A Joint Action Agenda for the United States and Pakistan.* Clinton Township, MI: Institute for Social Policy and Understanding, 2009.

Munir, Asad. "How FATA Was Won by the Taliban." *Express Tribune*, June 21, 2010.

Musharaf, Pervez. *In the Line of Fire: A Memoir.* New York: Simon and Schuster, 2006.

Nagl, John A. *Learning to Eat Soup with a Knife: Counterinsurgency Lessons from Malaya and Vietnam.* Chicago, IL: University of Chicago Press, 2005.

Nawaz, Shuja. *FATA – A Most Dangerous Place: Meeting the Challenge of Militancy and Terror in the Federally Administered Tribal Areas of Pakistan.* Washington DC: Center for Strategic & International Studies, 2009.

"North Waziristan Clerics to Launch 'Silent Protest'." *Daily Times*, August 3, 2007.

"Over 4,000 Houses Destroyed in Waziristan Operation: Report." *Dawn*, November 8, 2008.

"Pakistan and the Taliban: A Real Offensive or a Phony War?" *The Economist*, April 30, 2009.

"Pakistan Gets $256 Million for Support US." *Daily Times*, August 1, 2003.

"Pakistan Pays Tribe Al Qaeda Debt." *BBC News*, February 9, 2005.

"President Musharaf Address to the Nation." *The News*, March 8, 2002.

"President Musharaf Interview on PBS Documentary 'Frontline: The Return of the Taliban'." October 3, 2006.

Puri, Samir. *Pakistan's War on Terrorism: Strategies for Combating Jihadist Armed Groups Since 9/11*. New York: Routledge, 2012.

Qadir, Shaukat. "The State's Responses to the Pakistani Taliban Onslaught." In *Insurgency and Counterinsurgency in South Asia through a Peacebuilding Lens*, edited by Moeed Yusuf. Washington, DC: United States Institute of Peace, 2014.

Qazi, Shehzad H. "Rebels of the Frontier: Origins, Organization, and Recruitment of the Pakistani Taliban." *Small Wars & Insurgencies* 22, no. 4 (2011): 574–602.

Ramsay, Clay, Steven Kull, Stephen Weber, and Evan Lewis. "Pakistani Public Opinion on the Swat Conflict, Afghanistan, and the US." WorldPublicOpinion.org, 2008.

Rashid, Ahmed. "Pakistan's Worrisome Pullback." *The Washington Post*, June 6, 2008.

Rashid, Haroon. "Pakistan Taleban Vow More Violence." *BBC News*, January 29, 2007.

Richter, Paul, and Christi Parsons. "Obama Prepares to Meet with Leaders of Afghanistan, Pakistan." *Los Angeles Times*, May 5, 2009.

Riedel, Bruce. "Pakistan: The Critical Battlefield." *Current History* 107, no. 712 (2008): 358.

Sewall, Sarah. *The U.S. Army/Marine Corps Counterinsurgency Field Manual*. Chicago, IL: University of Chicago Press, 2007.

Shah, Aqil. "Pakistan After Musharraf: Praetorianism and Terrorism." *Journal of Democracy* 19, no. 4 (2008): 22.

Shahid, Shamim. "Baitullah, Supporters Lay Down Arms." *The Nation*, February 9, 2005.

Shahzad, Saleem. "The Knife at Pakistan's Throat." *Asia Times*, September 2, 2006.

Smith, M. L. R. "A Tradition That Never Was: Critiquing the Critique of British COIN." *Small Wars Journal* (2012).

"60 Miles from Islamabad, Editorial" *New York Times*, April 26, 2009.

"Soldier Killed in Pakistan Militant Attack." *Dawn*, July 26, 2007.

"Spotlight Falls on Taliban Man Accused of Murdering Benazir," *Daily Times*, January 28, 2008.

Sud, Hari. "Pakistan: Why Is Mushrraf Smiling These Days?" *South Asia Analysis Group, Paper No.* 1188 (2004).

"Taliban Attacks Double After Pakistan's Deal with Militants." *Guardian*, September 29, 2006.

Tohid, Owais. "The New Frontier." *Newsline* (Pakistan), April2004.

Trinuier, Roger. *Modern Warfare: A French View of Counterinsurgency*. New York: Praeger, 1964.

"U.S. Department of State, Congressional Budget Justification for Foreign Operations, Fiscal Year 2007," 2007. http://www.state.gov/documents/organization/60641.pdf.

Weinbaum, Marvin G. "Hard Choices in Countering Insurgency and Terrorism along Pakistan's North-West Frontier." *Journal of International Affairs* 63, no. 1 (2009): 75.

Weinstein, Jeremy M. *Inside Rebellion: The Politics of Insurgent Violence.* Cambridge: Cambridge University Press, 2007.

Yusufzai, Mushtaq. "Taliban Warns of Attack on Capital." *The News,* June 10, 2008.

Yusufzai, Rahimullah. "All Quiet on the North Western Front." *Newsline* (Pakistan), May 2004.

Yusufzai, Rahimullah, and Sailab Mahsud. "Troops Pull out of Azam Warsak Area." *The News,* March 29, 2004.

Zaidi, Syed ManzarAbbas. "The United States and the Counterinsurgency: The Peace Process in Pakistan." *American Foreign Policy Interests* 31, no. 3 (May 18, 2009): 149–165.

Zaidi, Syed Manzar Abbas. "Pakistan's Anti-Taliban Counter-Insurgency." *The RUSI Journal* 155, no. 1 (February 2010): 10–19.

4 Strong Counterinsurgency and Decline of the FATA Insurgency[1]

The Tehrik-i-Taliban Pakistan (TTP) insurgency seriously challenged the Pakistani government's writ of state in FATA from 2004 to 2008. This chapter argues that the execution of a better counterinsurgency operation staring from 2009 by the Pakistani government against the powerful FATA insurgency led to its decline around 2016. The effectiveness of counterinsurgency involved far more than simply a change in the amount of force used by the state. Accordingly, the execution of a better counterinsurgency since 2009 by the Pakistani government against the powerful FATA insurgency involved the transformation of forces from conventional ones to counterinsurgent ones, requiring a judicious use of force focusing on the destruction of insurgents' strength. This led to the insurgency's decline.

Growing TTP Threat

As discussed in the previous chapter, the Pakistani government's initially weak counterinsurgency campaign from 2004 to 2008, centered on various peace agreements, led to escalation of the FATA insurgency. As a result, the Pakistani Taliban not only succeeded in establishing effective control over certain agencies of FATA, such as Bajaur and North and South Waziristan, but also established influence in some settled parts of the country, such as Swat, which is only 170 kilometers from the country's capital, Islamabad.[2] The international community, especially the US, was alarmed by the growing power of the FATA insurgents because of their role in the ongoing insurgency in Afghanistan.[3]

The TTP's growing power posed a serious challenge to Pakistan's internal security. Some security analysts warned the Pakistani government of the seriousness of the TTP's threat to the country's stability. Ahmed Rahsid, for example, contended that "Pakistan's biggest threat comes from the Pakistani Taliban. It does not come from India."[4] Another security analyst, Hassan Abbas, commented, "Dismantling TTP and bringing its leadership to justice is critical for Pakistan's internal security."[5] The Obama's administration also pressured Pakistan to take effective steps in tackling the growing TTP strength.

DOI: 10.4324/9781003349259-4

The Obama Administration's New Approach Towards the Pakistan–Afghanistan Region

After the new administration in the US took office in January 2009, President Obama regarded the Pakistan–Afghanistan region as the epicentre of international terrorism and expressed his concern over the possibility of another attack against the US homeland might originate from this place. Therefore, the new administration intensified efforts to rout out terrorist groups in both countries. The US accelerated its counterinsurgency campaign against the Taliban insurgents in Afghanistan and pushed Pakistan hard for more effective efforts against Al Qaeda militants, and their local affiliates in the FATA.

Before Barack Obama assumed the presidential office, the insurgency in Afghanistan had become a far more serious threat than before. At that time, the US and NATO forces were heavily involved in fighting a resilient insurgency that had secured sustained support from the tribal region of Pakistan.[6] The Obama administration realized that Pakistan "was a necessary element of the military and counter-terrorism campaign in Afghanistan."[7]

President Obama announced the new US strategy, 'Af-Pak', toward Afghanistan and Pakistan on 27 March 2009.[8] President Obama had resolved to focus on the Pakistan–Afghanistan region more seriously, neglected under the previous administration.[9] Obama laid out his Af-Pak strategy with one "clear and focused goal": "to disrupt, dismantle, and defeat Al Qaeda in Pakistan and Afghanistan, and to prevent their return to either country in the future."[10] The Obama administration understood that problems in Afghanistan could not be resolved without addressing problems in Pakistan, as the future of both countries was "inextricably linked."[11] Therefore, the new administration announced that the two countries would be treated as part of "one theatre of operations for US diplomacy and one challenge for [Washington's] overall policy."[12] The tribal areas of Pakistan were identified as a serious concern because terrorist attacks across the world emanated from this region.[13] In Obama's words:

> ... I am convinced that our security is at stake in Afghanistan and Pakistan. This is the epicenter of violent extremism practiced by Al Qaeda. It is from here that we were attacked on 9/11, and it is from here that new attacks are being plotted as I speak. This is no idle danger; no hypothetical threat. In the last few months alone, we have apprehended extremists within our borders who were sent here from the border region of Afghanistan and Pakistan to commit new acts of terror. And this danger will only grow if the region slides backwards, and Al Qaeda can operate with impunity. We must keep the pressure on al Qaeda, and to do that, we must increase the stability and capacity of our partners in the region.[14]

While recognising the "mixed results" of Pakistan's performance in the war against terrorism, President Obama announced that America would not give

Pakistan a "blank cheque" in the future.[15] In outlining his new policy, President Obama pledged to provide the necessary support to the Pakistan government, contingent on the country's willingness to "eliminate the sanctuary enjoyed by Al Qaeda and other terrorist groups."[16] In addition, the Obama administration focused on enhancing the partnership through military and economic assistance.[17] To build Pakistan's capacity, the US Department of Defense allocated almost US$400 million to train and equip the paramilitary Frontier Corps (FC). In addition, an amount of US$3 billion was allocated over the next five years to train and equip Pakistan's army and paramilitary forces for counterinsurgency missions.[18]

Furthermore, the Obama administration also increased military supplies to Pakistan. In March 2010, the US delivered 14 AH-1Cobra gunship helicopters to the country.[19] Washington offered to supply Pakistan with an additional 14 F-16 C/D Block 52 fighter jets in addition to the previous 18 Block 52 F-16 aircrafts.[20] In June 2010, the Pakistani Air Force (PAF) received three F-16s. The provision of F-16s removed a long-standing impediment in US–Pakistani military ties.[21] The United States also offered to provide Pakistan with shadow drones for surveillance.[22] However, to ensure the continuation of the US military assistance, the Secretary of State needed to be sure that Pakistan "has demonstrated a sustained commitment to and is making significant efforts towards combating terrorist groups."[23]

Apart from enhancing Pakistan's counterinsurgency capabilities, the Af-Pak strategy emphasised the development of Pakistan's civilian sector as part of demonstrating its long-term commitment to the country. The Af-Pak strategy highlighted the "trust deficit" between the two countries, while stating that the US government "must engage the Pakistani people based on our long-term commitment to helping them build a stable economy, a stronger democracy, and a vibrant civil society."[24] Obama said:

> In the past, we too often defined our relationship with Pakistan narrowly. Those days are over. Moving forward, we are committed to a partnership with Pakistan that is built on a foundation of mutual interest, mutual respect and mutual trust.[25]

The core of the new US policy for Pakistan, manifested through the Enhanced Partnership Act 2009 (also known as the Kerry–Lugar Bill), aimed at tripling US economic assistance to Pakistan to US$1.5 billion a year between 2010 and 2014.[26]

The Obama administration also considered Pakistan's less-than impressive performance and unsatisfactory assistance in the war on terrorism. It kept up pressure on Pakistan to expedite its efforts against terrorism by pointing out that actions should be taken indiscriminately against all kinds of terrorist groups. In November 2009, the US National Security Advisor James Jones delivered President Obama's letter to Pakistan President Asif Ali Zardari, warning that Pakistan's policy of using some terrorist groups to gain regional objectives "cannot continue," and calling for "closer collaboration against all extremist groups, including Al Qaeda, the Afghan Taliban, the Haqqani network, Lashkar-e-Taiba, and the TTP."[27] The Obama administration perceived that the weakening of the Pakistan-based terrorist groups "will pose less of a direct threat to US, Indian, or Afghan interests. They will become less relevant to Pakistan's own regional strategic calculations."[28] To motivate Pakistan to take on these militant groups, President Obama assured Pakistan in the same letter of "an expanded strategic partnership", including "an effort to help reduce tensions between Pakistan and India."[29]

Furthermore, Obama's strategy brought a significant change in the US-led counterinsurgency campaign in Afghanistan. The strategy emphasised using "all elements of international power – diplomatic, informational, military and economic"[30] in addition to the use of military force, to achieve the core strategic objective of defeating Al Qaeda and its allies in Afghanistan. Subsequently, the Obama administration increased US troops in Afghanistan under the troop surge policy. The first increase was announced in March 2009, consisting of 21,000 troops (including 17,000 combat troops) supplemented by another major increase of 30,000 more troops in December 2009.[31] Washington was quite determined not to allow the Taliban to capture power in Afghanistan.[32] President Obama's hard stance, followed by a better counterinsurgency approach in Afghanistan, helped shape Pakistan's counterinsurgency approach in the FATA.

The Obama administration also increased US drone strikes in the FATA region to target Al Qaeda and its allies.[33] The Obama administration clearly realised that the insurgency in Afghanistan could not be controlled without eliminating its support base in the FATA.[34] President Obama marked the FATA region as "the most dangerous place in the world."[35] A significant increase in drone strikes in FATA aimed at in destroying the terrorists' safe havens without waiting for Islamabad to act. According to Fair, Washington increased drone strikes in Pakistan because of the unsatisfactory performance of the country in the war against terrorism and its continued relationship with the Afghan Taliban groups.[36]

Obama ordered his first drone strike in Pakistan within two days of taking the presidential oath.[37] Reportedly, 44 drone strikes had occurred in the tribal areas of Pakistan between 2004 and 2008, during the second term of President George W. Bush.[38] In contrast, during President Obama's first year in office alone, 53 drone strikes targeted the tribal region, with another 118 drone attacks recorded in 2010.[39] The US drone attacks in the tribal areas such as South and North Waziristan and other agencies led to the death of several Al Qaeda and Taliban leaders, including Baitullah Mehsud, who had emerged as a hard-core insurgent leader against Pakistan.

As a result of this increased pressure amid the US Af-Pak strategy, Pakistan intensified its counterinsurgency campaign in the FATA.[40] In October 2009, Pakistani security forces launched a major operation in South Waziristan against the TTP, which significantly damaged the organisation's training and military capabilities. The military operations have continued since early 2010 and been extended to other agencies of the FATA. In addition, Pakistan launched an intensive counterinsurgency campaign in North Waziristan in June 2014, which emerged as the last sanctuary of Al Qaeda militants and other Pakistan-based terrorist groups. As a result of sustained and better counterinsurgency efforts by the Pakistani state, the TTP hold was broken in the FATA.

Pakistan's Effective Counterinsurgency

The Pakistani government made significant changes in its counterinsurgency strategy to make the campaign more effective beginning in 2009. For example, the military forces fighting in FATA underwent a significant transformation, from conventional to counterinsurgent. The forces were given appropriate modern counterinsurgency training and equipment. The transformation of the fighting forces was followed by the targeted use of force against insurgents, focusing on destroying their infrastructure and avoiding civilian damages. Local people were evacuated from the insurgency-stricken areas before military strikes were launched. The precise and effective use of force destroyed the insurgents' sanctuaries and, most importantly, crippled their military capabilities. Their waning fighting capability forced them to run, which allowed the military forces to capture and hold the area, stationing military troops to reduce the chances of the insurgents' return. These strategies quite successfully defeated the TTP, forcing the leadership to seek sanctuary across the border in Afghanistan.

A Strong Political Will

Political will plays an important role in making a counterinsurgency campaign successful.[41] Political will is demonstrated by how the government deals with insurgency at strategic and operational levels, which requires the appropriation of sufficient resources. For example, David Galula contends that counterinsurgency operations "require a large concentration of efforts, resources, and personnel."[42] Similarly Paul Dixon observes that a strong political is indispensable for a successful counterinsurgency.[43] Allocation of necessary resources to defeat an insurgency is possible when backed by a strong political will.[44]

The Pakistani state's strong political will to defeat the FATA insurgency was a direct response to the exponential increase in the strength and influence of the TTP in FATA and beyond. Also, the TTP's increasing involvement in terrorist attacks in mainland Pakistan led to a shift in the government's perception of threat to the country towards the FATA insurgency and away from India.[45] In an interview with the German magazine *Der Spiegel*, General Shuja Pasha, the head of Pakistan's chief spy agency, Inter-Services Intelligence, said, "Terror is our enemy, not India."[46] This shift was evident throughout the military's culture.[47] And Pakistan's prime minister, Yousuf Raza Gilani, termed the war against insurgents "a war of the country's survival."[48]

The shift in threat perception was accompanied by a change in public mood, which was turning against the TTP. After numerous large-scale terrorist attacks by TTP militants in mosques and marketplaces across the country, public opinion turned significantly against the Pakistani Taliban movement.[49] Public opinion further swung behind the government after the group declared Pakistan's constitution un-Islamic. This fostered the popular perception that the Pakistani offensive was driven by the growing insurgent threat, not by pressure from the US.[50]

The majority of Pakistanis therefore demanded military operations against the TTP. An opinion poll in 2009 put anti-TTP sentiment among the Pakistani public at 81%.[51] In a Pew Research poll in August 2009, 77% of Pakistanis supported military operations against the Pakistani Taliban.[52] Some religious political parties, such as Jamiat-ul-Ulema-Pakistan and Ahl-e-Sunnat, also voiced support of military operations against the TTP militants.[53] Breyman and Salman reported that "growing revulsion against the Pakistani Taliban's outrageous behavior is one of the major factors underlying improved public support for the Army's counterinsurgency offensives."[54] This wider political and popular support gave the Pakistani government much-needed legitimacy in planning and executing a better counterinsurgency campaign.

The Pakistani state's growing political will became evident when negotiations with the insurgents were dropped. The negotiations had only strengthened the insurgents' hold. Zaidi observes that "the realization had perhaps dawned on government circles that the negotiation process had not yielded many dividends."[55] Highlighting a change in the government's stance toward the militants, he noted that "the continuous peace deals and their unilateral revocation by the militants sapped the negotiating will of the government, which banned the Tehrik-i-Taliban [Pakistan]."[56]

Strong political will translated into effective action against the insurgents. For example, the military operation in Bajaur Agency was conducted with improved planning and more force than previous military operations in FATA.[57] More than 20,000 troops took part, assisted by helicopter gunships, tanks, artillery, and about 3,000 local fighters.[58] Zaidi noted that "the Bajaur operation was pursued much more vigorously than previous ones had been."[59]

Similarly, significant military resources were devoted to defeat the insurgents in South Waziristan. The "intensity of efforts and vastness of means are essential" to show resoluteness on the part of the counterinsurgents.[60] The military operations in 2009 were carried out with better planning and resources, fielding 30,000–60,000 troops.[61] The Pakistani army diverted some troops, including seven combat brigades, from the Indian border and deployed them in South Waziristan to support the counterinsurgency operations.[62] The FATA insurgency was being treated as the country's most important security threat, even surpassing India, at least momentarily.

The June 2014 military operation in North Waziristan, Operation Zarb-e-Azb, was also conducted vigorously after peace talks with militants had been given a chance. The democratic government newly elected in 2013 and led by Prime Minister Nawaz Sharif had announced peace negotiations with the Pakistani Taliban.[63] But the insurgents were not willing to lay down their arms, and they continued their terrorist activities. In a spectacular terrorist act, the militants attacked Jinnah International Airport in Karachi on June 8, 2014, killing 36 people.[64] The government launched a full military operation on June 15.[65] Military spokesperson General Asim Bajwa marked the operation as a "war of survival," adding, "this is the biggest and most well-coordinated operation ever conducted against terrorists."[66] Military troops, the Frontier Corps (a paramilitary force), intelligence operatives, and the Pakistan Air Force jointly conducted the operation in North Waziristan. At the heart of Operation Zarb-e-Azb was the 7th Infantry Division, considered the Pakistani army's "oldest and the most battle-hardened division."[67] Two battalions of Special Services Group, the army's special operations force, also took part. As a result of these far more dedicated operations, the military was finally successful in routing the TTP from its strongholds in Bajaur and North and South Waziristan.

Improving the Military Forces' Counterinsurgency Training and Skills

A strong political will alone is not sufficient to make a counterinsurgency campaign successful. ounterinsurgency training is required for a military victory against insurgents because conventional force is counterproductive in fighting an insurgency.[68] It requires conventional forces to adapt its organizational structure and strategy in line with the counterinsurgency operation.[69] Specific training is also required.[70] In this regard, the British document on counterinsurgency, *Keeping the Peace (Duties in Support of Civil Power)*, stated that "there is no place for a rigid mind.... Although the principles of war generally remain the same, the ability to adapt and improvise is essential."[71] These changes are necessary because counterinsurgency warfare differs from conventional warfare in its objectives. A conventional war pursues decisive strategic goals, whereas counterinsurgency aims more at overt political objectives.[72] Writing in the mid-1980s, Eliot Cohen highlighted that counterinsurgency campaigns are "not 'half' a war, but rather a completely different kind of conflict."[73] Apart from the military forces, the role of local security forces such as the police is considered a crucial element in a counterinsurgency campaign, because these forces tend to have a better understanding of the threat environment and local intelligence.[74]

Pakistani military elites now had a clear understanding that the military forces lacked counterinsurgency skills, which explained their poor and inefficient performance against the insurgents from 2004 to 2008. General Ashfaq

Kiani, then chief of the armed forces, focused on improving the counterinsurgency strategy through new arms procurement choices and a revised military curriculum. Calling 2008 the "Year of the Soldier" and 2009 the "Year of Training," Kiani also initiated reforms in the Directorate of Military Operations (the army's strategy think tank) and intelligence operations to meet the needs of counterinsurgency warfare.[75] The Frontier Corps was given counterinsurgency training, plus modern counterinsurgency weapons, along with better salary packages and promotions.[76] These measures transformed the corps into a modern fighting force appropriate for counterinsurgency.[77]

In 2009, the Pakistani government also accepted counterinsurgency training assistance from the US.[78] The US Special Forces personnel conducted counterinsurgency training for Frontier Corps officers.[79] The Pakistani military leadership had previously refused such help from the US. Military officials had questioned the utility of counterinsurgency training, saying that the country's main security threats emanated from India, not from the TTP. But with the shift in threat perception, Pakistan's counterinsurgency capabilities were being significantly enhanced. A US intelligence assessment affirmed the considerable improvement in Pakistan's counterinsurgency approach: "Pakistan has added more border posts, begun counter-insurgency training, fenced portions of the border and seeks to obtain counter-insurgency equipment while also expanding para-military forces."[80] These adaptations enhanced the forces' capabilities to better fight the insurgents and ultimately defeat them.

The Pakistani military also improved its counterinsurgency approach through "learning by doing."[81] Based on the experience of the Bajaur counterinsurgency operations during Operation Shirdil ("Lion Heart") in August 2008, junior officers were made part of the decision-making process – especially Frontier Corps officers, who had traditionally been considered incompetent because of their training and due to their ethnic links with the predominantly Pashtun militants.[82] Input from junior officers in the field led Lt. Gen. Tariq Khan, the commander of the operation, to change his approach to the counterinsurgency considerably. Instead of employing an enemy-centric "out-terrorizing the terrorist" model, Tariq used a population security approach, emphasizing troop patrols and supporting tribal *lashkars* (militias) and *jirgas* (tribal councils).[83] The best counterinsurgency practices advocate "deploying smaller and more dispersed units, patrolling to protect the population, and raising local police forces to sustain operational gains."[84]

"Learning by doing" through battleground experience and significant input from junior officers brought about radical change from the pre-2008 Pakistani counterinsurgency campaigns in the tribal areas. The newly acquired tactics and better use of human intelligence enabled a more judicious use of force to protect the civilian population. The local population of Bajaur was evacuated to enable airpower and heavy artillery, forcing militants from their hideouts.[85] After attacking the insurgents' forces with intensive airstrikes and artillery fire, ground forces were mobilized to chase and apprehend them.[86] Learning in the field significantly improved counter-insurgency tactics, which in turn helped dry up the insurgents' local support base, making it easier to apprehend the insurgents without alienating the local population.

Targeted Use of Force to Avoid Collateral Damage

Adaptation of conventional force to counterinsurgency force encourages a more judicious use of force, not only effectively targeting insurgents but also helping to reduce civilian damage. Andrew Mumford contends that "the traditional 'centre of gravity' for a counter-insurgency campaign is the population," which requires that "plans for military assaults upon the enemy have been couched in terms of protecting the civilian population and preserving their trust."[87] Similarly, Rod Thornton maintains that in counter-insurgency campaigns, "the quality of force ... has to be seen as more important than its quantity."[88] Indiscriminate or excessive use of force in a counterinsurgency campaign tends to aggravate the grievances of the local population.[89] In addition, a firepower-intensive approach in a counter-insurgency campaign is seldom productive. Samarjit Ghosh contended that "the use of brute force instead of low-intensity strikes is a classic flaw in counterinsurgency campaigns: its military effectiveness is suspect, and it invariably embitters the local population."[90] The security of the local population is particularly important. Paul Dixon suggests a less coercive approach to counterinsurgency, using "minimum force" to avoid civilian damage.[91]

From mid-August 2008, the Pakistani military adopted a counter-insurgency approach, shifting from the indiscriminate use of force to more targeted use to protect the civilian population.[92] Often, the local population was cleared out to separate them from the insurgents and to achieve the targeted use of force. After isolating the population, the Pakistani military used air power to soften up the insurgents' targets, followed by ground forces to secure the area. Haider Mullick contended that Pakistan "has made a significant but tenuous move toward a hybrid approach that relies on killing the enemy but minimizing collateral damage."[93]

Operation Sherdil in Bajaur saw improved strategy and planning, with the targeted use of force significantly reducing collateral damage. But it also increased the troops' vulnerability, leading to higher Pakistani military casualties.[94] At the same time, however, the Frontier Corps emerged as a more competent and useful localized force, able to strike the fleeing insurgents more effectively without alienating the local population.[95]

The Pakistani military launched Operation Rah-e-Nijat (Path of Salvation) on October 17, 2009, with the stated objectives of securing population centers and dismantling the TTP organizational infrastructure in South Waziristan.[96] The military tried to limit collateral damage by evacuating the population before the attack and by using tactics learned through local experience.[97] For two months before the ground assault, a blockade was imposed around the target area to cut off the insurgents' supply lines. Intelligence resources rooted in the area were used to target air strikes on the insurgents' sanctuaries and infrastructure.[98]

The military also used psychological techniques to isolate the TTP militants from the larger population. Leaflets from local religious authorities and tribes were circulated, informing the youth of "false jihad" and blaming the militants for bringing destruction to the tribal areas. A letter was sent from the chief of army staff, General Ashfaq Kayani, to the tribal elders of the Mehsud tribe, explaining that the operation was aimed at local and foreign militants, not at the Mehsud.[99] A security analyst maintained that "the focus on conducting psychological and information operations, amassing popular support, and dividing insurgents to limit the scope of operations all factored into the moderately successful outcome."[100]

The targeted use of force helped limit collateral damage.[101] Major General Athar Abbas, the chief military spokesman, said, "We are trying to shape the environment before we move in for the fight. We are also trying to minimize the loss of life."[102] Almost 200,000 locals had been relocated in South Waziristan, and some locals complained that the government's arrangements to deal with the displaced people were inadequate. Similarly, before launching the military operation in North Waziristan in June 2014, the government had deliberately evacuated the local population to protect them and to minimize collateral damage.[103]

Eliminating Insurgents' Infrastructure, Clear and Hold Strategy

A true victory against an insurgency cannot be achieved without dismantling the insurgents' infrastructure, including their political, economic, and military capabilities. And after any victory, troops must be stationed in the area to prevent the insurgents' return. Paul Melshen argued that "if the infrastructure is not destroyed, the insurgent organization will either survive as it is, or adapt to the current counterinsurgent pressures on the organization."[104] Timothy Deady claims that destruction of "insurgents' strategic and operational centers of gravity" permitted the US forces to achieve successful counterinsurgency in Philippines.[105] After destroying the insurgents' infrastructure, clearing the area of the remnants of the insurgency is also essential. Clearing requires the counterinsurgency forces to find and destroy scores of improvised explosive devices and frequently engage in house-to-house or field-to-field fighting.[106] Even after clearing, there is a need to hold the area to prevent the insurgents' returning.[107]

During the counterinsurgency campaign, Pakistani military forces focused on eliminating the insurgents' infrastructure. Operation Sherdil, which began in Bajaur in August 2008, aimed to target, and dismantle the nerve center of the TTP there. The military succeeded in destroying the insurgents' hideouts and other infrastructure. They also recovered large stockpiles of weapons, ammunition, and other materials, such as guerrilla warfare manuals and bomb-making instructions.[108] After eliminating the insurgents' military strength, the forces conducted search operations to apprehend the fleeing militants.[109] After seizing control of the Taliban-dominated areas in Bajuar, the military held the area, maintaining a permanent presence with small bases and troop patrols to prevent the return of the militants.

The military faced serious challenges while conducting military operations in South Waziristan. The TTP there was considered highly adept in guerrilla warfare. And a sizeable number of Punjabi Taliban and Uzbek fighters had reinforced the TTP and its ability to resist the military. One Pakistani military official noted, "It's going to be a tough fight for these places."[110]

Despite these difficulties, the Pakistani military made significant progress against the insurgents in South Waziristan in October and November of 2009 and wrested back control of important towns and villages. The operations targeted TTP strongholds such as Ladha, Makin, and Sararogha, which had served as the command-and-control center of the TTP militants.[111] After stiff resistance, the military finally gained control of these areas. The houses of militant commanders, such as Wali-ur-Rehaman and Shabeeb Khan, and other suspects were also demolished.[112] The insurgents' sanctuaries were completely wiped out. By January 2010, Pakistani forces had cleared most of the South Waziristan Agency of insurgents. Athar Abbas announced military victory, saying, "The myth has been broken that this was a graveyard for empires, and it would be a graveyard for the Army."[113] The holding tactics were repeated in South Waziristan: after dismantling the insurgents' infrastructure and seizing control of the Taliban-dominated areas, military troops were stationed there to prevent the return of the insurgents.

Similarly, during Operation Zarb-e-Azb in North Waziristan in June 2014, the Pakistani Air Force used airstrikes to destroy the militants' military capability. Precision-targeted weapons destroyed the insurgents' infrastructure and weakened their overall capability. The military recovered a huge cache of weapons and ammunition. According to the commander of the operation, Major General Zafar Ullah Khan, the arms recovered from the militants could have supported the conflict for another 15 years.[114] After the first year of Operation Zarb-e-Azb, North Waziristan was believed to be largely free from insurgent control. Pakistan's army chief, General Raheel Sharif, said, "We have successfully dismantled their infrastructure and created significant effects. We as a nation are determined to take this surge to its logical end, whatever it may take."[115] A Pakistani newspaper reported, "The stronghold of the notorious Haqqani Network and TTP is no longer their command-and-control center. The combined air and land offensive has decimated the sanctuary."[116]

After destroying the insurgents' infrastructure, clearing the area of the remnants of insurgency is essential. Pakistan's counterinsurgency approach used a "clear and hold" strategy. Haider Mullick noted that Pakistan's counterinsurgency strategy had "executed a presence-oriented approach":

they "cleared areas, [and] established small bases inside populated areas (instead of going back to large forward operating bases)."[117] After clearing an area, the Pakistani troops stationed there provided support to local intelligence and militias for continued success. After defeating the insurgents in North Waziristan, the government announced it would garrison the area to prevent the return of insurgents. Army chief General Raheel Sharif said that the "army won't go back from the area till the job is done."[118] The military also deployed troops to forward positions in mountainous and forested terrain, such as Shawal and Dattakhel, to attack the fleeing insurgents.[119]

Socioeconomic Development as Part of Counterinsurgency Strategy

After the destruction of the insurgency infrastructure, winning over the local population is required for a durable success in a counterinsurgency. Mostly an insurgency is largely motivated by social, political, or economic grievances, therefore, defeating an insurgency requires more than a military approach. Galula contends that "counterinsurgency is 80 percent political action and only 20 percent military."[120] This can be achieved primarily by improving governance through social and economic development.[121] By addressing grievances through initiating development projects such as building schools, roads, or health clinics, the counterinsurgents to win over the population, which in turn tends to help undermine insurgents' cause. The British counterinsurgency expert Sir Robert Thompson said that "'winning' the population can tritely be summed up as good government in all its aspects ... such as improved health measures and clinics ... new schools ... and improved livelihood and standard of living."[122] A retired US Marine, T. X. Hammes, said emphatically, "The fundamental weapon in counterinsurgency is good governance."[123] In addition, to reclaim government sovereignty and legitimacy in an area that was once under the control of an insurgent group, the government must "re-establish institutions and local security forces" and focus on "rebuilding infrastructure and basic services" to establish "local governance and the rule of law."[124]

On the front of introducing socioeconomic development in the region, Pakistan's counterinsurgency campaign did not perform well. For the social and economic development of the FATA region, the government launched the Sustainable Development Plan.[125] The government also tasked the FATA Secretariat, a FATA Task Force, and the FATA Development Authority to identify the development needs of the region and to develop short, medium, and long-term strategies to meet them. But many of these plans were not fully implemented, mainly because of insufficient resources.[126]

After defeating the insurgents militarily, the Pakistani government launched various development projects to address the grievances of the population. However, these attempts largely failed. For instance, after clearing areas of insurgents in Bajaur in 2010, the military undertook various development projects, such as building schools and local health units. The government also initiated projects to develop road infrastructure in the agency and helped the local people in building houses and in setting up businesses.[127] But locals complained of inadequate funding compared to the scale of destruction from military operations.

In some cases, such as the South and North Waziristan Agencies, the situation was far worse. Because of the heavy presence of the insurgents in both agencies, full-fledged military operations were launched. These two agencies had witnessed a huge displacement of the local population, as well as the massive destruction of peoples' houses and property, because the fighting between the insurgents and the government forces was so intense.[128] A large number of local people had to leave their houses when the security forces launched the Rah-i-Nijat operation in the Mehsud-dominated area of South Waziristan in 2009.[129]

Similarly, the June 2014 Operation Zarb-e-Azb in North Waziristan displaced around two million local people, almost 70% of whom were women and children.[130] The government was ill-prepared and ill-equipped to deal with the scale of this humanitarian crisis.[131] Conditions at the camps established for the internally displaced people were miserable; they lacked basic infrastructure such as water, electricity, washrooms, and proper living arrangements.[132] The lack of civilian-led governance in FATA made the situation more challenging and increased the vulnerability of the displaced people.

In early 2015, the military claimed to have eliminated the insurgents from their last refuge in North Waziristan. In March and April of the same year, the Pakistani government announced a strategy for repatriation and rehabilitation of the people of FATA. The rehabilitation strategy aimed to reconstruct damaged facilities, particularly those dealing with education and health, and improve local governance. For the rehabilitation of internally displaced people, the government provided Rs. 5 billion (US$ 33.33 Million) to the FATA Secretariat.[133] But the local people complained that they could not rebuild their homes with the little money provided by the government and did not have adequate means to start a new life in FATA.[134] The people who returned to their homes faced serious hardships, with a poorly performing agricultural sector, few employment opportunities, and dysfunctional businesses and markets.[135]

As FATA was directly controlled by the federal government, it lacked the institutional capacity to plan and execute development projects. However, in May 2018 the government of Pakistan passed the 31st Amendment to the constitution, merging FATA with the adjacent province of Khyber-Pakhtunkhwa.[136] Mainstreaming FATA and giving its people the same economic and political rights as any other province of the country may help address the long-held grievances. Without true amelioration of the socioeconomic conditions of the people, a permanent peace in the region cannot be guaranteed. Brigadier (Retd.) Shaukat Qadir maintained that "the virtual absence of a holistic governance response to the counterinsurgency strategy leaves a vacuum that, if left unfilled, would doom the state's efforts to pacify militants permanently."[137]

Collapse of the TTP

As a result of the more effective counterinsurgency of the Pakistani government, the TTP's hold in FATA was broken. As discussed earlier, the TTP's
hold and infrastructure were dismantled in the FATA and the Pakistani
government established its writ of state. The military operation also significantly reduced the operational capability of the TTP, as evidenced by the
reduction of terrorist-related incidents in Pakistani cities, particularly in
FATA. For example, 2,863 people were killed in such incidents in FATA in
2014, but only 411 in the first three months of 2015.[138]

The ongoing and more effective assaults on the TTP have led to factionalism
and instability within the organization. Fazlullah emerged as the new leader of
the TTP amid a leadership crisis caused by the death of Hakimullah Mehsud in
a drone strike in November 2013. But Fazlullah did not gain wide popularity
within the ranks, because he did not belong to the Wazir or the Mehsud tribe,
unlike all previous leaders of the TTP. Since Fazlullah assumed the leadership,
the TTP has faced a number of factional conflicts. The factionalism worsened
after military strikes in June 2014. In September of that year, several leaders of
the TTP formed a new faction called Jamaat-ul Ahrar.[139] In October, several
other leaders broke away from Fazlullah's TTP and pledged allegiance to the
head of the Islamic State, Abu Bakr al-Baghdadi.[140]

In the face of territorial losses and internal factionalism, the TTP made
several missteps. In particular, attacking soft targets backfired. On December
16, 2014, militants belonging to a TTP faction led by Fazlullah attacked the
Army Public School in Peshawar, killing school children and staff members.
This attack was called "Pakistan's 9/11."[141] According to Michael Semple, a
former deputy European Union envoy to Afghanistan and an expert on the
Taliban, "Fazlullah's latest outrage reflects his weakness."[142] Another attack
was carried out at the Pakistan–India border crossing near Wagah, Lahore,
on November 2, 2014, by Jamaat ul-Ahrar, killing around 55 people.[143] An
attack in early 2016 at the Bacha Khan University in Charsadda, 20 miles
from Peshawar, by a faction of the TTP led by Mullah Mansoor, killed 20
people, including students and teachers.[144] These attacks demonstrate a deep
frustration within TTP ranks over its huge losses from the Zarb-e-Azb
campaign in North Waziristan.[145]

Due to the lack of cooperation between Pakistan and Afghanistan, and to
Afghanistan's lack of complete control over its territory, the Afghan pro-
vinces adjacent to FATA have become sanctuaries for the militants fleeing
the Zarb-e-Azb offensive. These safe havens have enabled the militants' leadership to survive and to continue plotting terrorist attacks within Pakistan.

Conclusion

The TTP's increasing hold in FATA and its indiscriminate terrorist attacks
prompted the Pakistani government to deal with the threat seriously. The US

pressure under the Obama administration was instrumental in pushing Pakistan to alter the counterinsurgency approach to deal with the TTP threat. This produced the strong political will necessary for decisive action against the TTP insurgency. With this strong resolve, the government came up with a better counterinsurgency strategy, which focused on specialized counterinsurgency training for the military forces. In addition, considerable military and financial resources were devoted to preparing the forces to launch attacks on the insurgents.

More troops, with more sophisticated weapons, enabled the military to destroy the insurgents' sanctuaries and their military capability. Most importantly, the "clear and hold" model was followed to consolidate the gains made against the insurgents: after clearing an area, troops were permanently stationed there to prevent the insurgents' return. But local communities were very unhappy with the large-scale destruction wrought by the military operations and the government's inadequate help with repatriation and rehabilitation. The Pashtun Tahafuz Movement (PTM) emerged in response to the grievances of the local communities.

To address these grievances, the government ended the semi-autonomous status of FATA by merging it with the neighboring province of Khyber-Pakhtunkhwa to bring the long-neglected region up to par with the rest of Pakistan. But it will take a great deal of time, resources, and, most importantly, strong government commitment to bring social and economic development to the region, which is imperative to prevent the resurgence of insurgency. Unless the long-standing socio-economic grievances of the local communities are addressed, the threat of insurgency will continue to haunt officials in Pakistan. The next chapter discusses the current situation of FATA after two decades of insurgency and counterinsurgency operations.

Notes

1 A version of this chapter is published as a Journal article. Shahzad Akhtar, "Decline of Insurgency in Pakistan's FATA: A Counterinsurgency Perspective," *Asian Survey* 54, no. 4 (2019).
2 See the editorial "60 Miles from Islamabad," *New York Times*, April 26, 2009.
3 Paul Richter Parsons and Christi Parsons, "Obama Prepares to Meet with Leaders of Afghanistan, Pakistan," *Los Angeles Times*, May 5, 2009.
4 Ahmed Rashid, "Pakistan's Continued Failure to Adopt a Counterinsurgency Strategy," *CTC Sentinel* 2, no. 3 (March 2009).
5 Hassan Abbas, "A Profile of Tehrik-i-Taliban Pakistan," *CTC Sentinel* 1, no.2 (January 2008): 4.
6 M.W. Aslam, "Understanding the 'Pak' in 'AfPak': The Obama Administration's Security Policy for Pakistan at the Mid-Term," *Journal of Policing, Intelligence and Counter Terrorism* 7, no. 1 (2012): 3.
7 Richard L. Armitage, Samuel R. Berger, and Daniel S. Markey, *U.S. Strategy for Pakistan and Afghanistan (Independent Task Force Report No. 65)* (New York and Washington, DC: Council on Foreign Relations, 2010), 29.
8 Ishtiaq Ahmad, "The U.S. Af-Pak Strategy: Challenges and Opportunities for Pakistan," *Asian Affairs: An American Review* 37, no. 4 (2010): 193.

9   K. Alan Kronstadt, *Pakistan–US Relations* (Congressional Research Service, Report No. *RL33498*, 2009), accessed on September 13, 2016, http://www.fas.org/sgp/crs/row/RL33498.pdf.

10   "Obama's Strategy for Afghanistan and Pakistan, March 2009," *Council on Foreign Relations*, accessed August 31, 2016, http://www.cfr.org/pakistan/obama s-strategy-afghanistan-pakistan-march-2009/p18952.

11   "Obama's Strategy for Afghanistan and Pakistan."

12   Quoted in K. Alan Kronstadt, *Pakistan: Key Current Issues and Developments* (Congressional Research Service Report No. *R41307*, 2010), 5–6, accessed on June 17, 2016, https://www.fas.org/sgp/crs/row/R41307.pdf.

13   "Obama's Strategy for Afghanistan and Pakistan, March 2009."

14   Quoted in Isaac Kfir, "U.S. Policy Toward Pakistan and Afghanistan under the Obama Administration," *The Middle East Review of International Affairs* 13, no. 4 (December 2009).

15   "Obama's Strategy for Afghanistan and Pakistan, March 2009."

16   White House, "White Paper of the Interagency Policy Group's Report on US Policy towards Afghanistan and Pakistan," *Washington, DC*, March 2009, accessed on March 15, 2016. https://www.whitehouse.gov/assets/documents/Afghanistan-Pakistan_White_Paper.pdf.

17   Ahmad, "The U.S. Af-Pak Strategy," 206.

18   Daniel Markey, *From AfPak to PakAf: A Response to the New US Strategy for South Asia* (Washington DC: Council on Foreign Relations, 2009), 2.

19   "US Delivers Cobra Gunships to Pakistan," *Nation*, March 17, 2010.

20   "PAF Ready to Thwart Indian Designs: Air Chief," *The News*, March 28, 2010.

21   Zahid Gishkori, "Pakistan Receives Three New F-16s," *Express Tribune*, June 27, 2010.

22   "Pak to Get 18 F-16s, Shadow Drones Likely Within a Year," *The Indian Express*, March 30, 2010.

23   Cited in Paul D. Miller, "How to Exercise U.S. Leverage Over Pakistan," *The Washington Quarterly* 35, no. 4 (2012): 38.

24   White House, "White Paper of the Interagency Policy Group's Report."

25   Kronstadt, "Pakistan: Key Current Issues and Developments," 8.

26   Miller, "How to Exercise U.S. Leverage Over Pakistan," 38.

27   Karen De Young, "U.S. Offers New Role for Pakistan: A Broader Partnership," *The Washington Post*, November 30, 2009.

28   Armitage, Berger, and Markey, *U.S. Strategy for Pakistan and Afghanistan (Independent Task Force Report No. 65)*, 33.

29   De Young, "U.S. Offers New Role for Pakistan."

30   White House, "White Paper of the Interagency Policy Group's Report."

31   Ahmad, "The U.S. Af-Pak Strategy," 195.

32   Kfir, "U.S. Policy Toward Pakistan and Afghanistan."

33   Peter Bergen and Katherine Tiedemann, *Revenge of the Drones: An Analysis of Drone Strikes in Pakistan* (Washington, DC: New America Foundation, 2009).

34   Aslam, "Understanding the 'Pak' in 'AfPak': The Obama Administration's Security Policy for Pakistan at the Mid-Term," 13.

35   Quoted in Kfir, "U.S. Policy Toward Pakistan and Afghanistan."

36   C. Christine Fair, "Time for Sober Realism: Renegotiating U.S. Relations with Pakistan," *The Washington Quarterly* 32, no. 2 (2009): 164.

37   James Joyner, "Obama Orders Pakistan Drone Attacks," *Atlantic Council*, January 24, 2009, accessed on June 15, 2016, http://www.atlanticcouncil.org/blogs/new-atlanticist/obama-orders-pakistan-drone-attacks.

38   Peter Bergen and Katherine Tiedemann, "Washington's Phantom War: The Effects of the U.S. Drone Program in Pakistan," *Foreign Affairs* 90, no. 4 (2011): 12–18; New America Foundation, *The Year of the Drone: An Analysis of*

US Drone Strikes in Pakistan, 2004–2011 (Washington DC: New America Foundation, 2011).

39 New America Foundation, *The Year of the Drone: An Analysis of US Drone Strikes in Pakistan.*

40 Ahmad, "The U.S. Af-Pak Strategy," 196.

41 M. L. R. Smith, "A Tradition That Never Was: Critiquing the Critique of British COIN," *Small Wars Journal* (2012).

42 David Galula, *Counterinsurgency Warfare: Theory and Practice* (Westport, CT: Praeger Security International, 2006), 55.

43 Paul Dixon, "Hearts and Minds? British Counterinsurgency from Malay to Iraq," *Journal of Strategic Studies* 32, no. 3 (2009): 357.

44 David H. Ucko and Robert Egnell, *Counterinsurgency in Crisis: Britain and the Challenges of Modern Warfare* (New York: Colombia University Press, 2013), 16.

45 Haider Ali Hussin Mullick, *Helping Pakistan Defeat the Taliban: A Joint Action Agenda for the United States and Pakistan* (Institute for Social Policy and Understanding, 2009), 6.

46 Susanne Koelbl, "Pakistan's New Intelligence Chief: Terror Is Our Enemy, Not India," *Der Spiegel,* January 6, 2009.

47 Interview, Maj. Gen. (retd.) Athar Abbas, Rawalpindi, Pakistan, April 5, 2014. Abbas was director-general of Inter-Services Public Relations, the media wing of the Pakistani Army, from 2008 to 2012.

48 Ishtiaq Mahsud, "Desperation in Pakistani Hospitals, Refugee Camps," *Associated Press,* May 9, 2009.

49 Mukhtar A. Khan, "Pakistani Government Offensive in Swat Heading for the Taliban of Waziristan," *Terrorism Monitor* 7, no. 17 (June 2009): 10.

50 Imtiaz Ali, "Military Victory in South Waziristan or the Beginning of a Long War," *Terrorism Monitor* 38, no. 202 (2009): 1–10.

51 Clay Ramsay, Steven Kull, Stephen Weber, and Evan Lewis, *Pakistani Public Opinion on the Swat Conflict, Afghanistan, and the US* (Washington, DC: The University of Maryland, 2009).

52 Pew Global Attitudes Project, *Pakistani Public Opinion: Growing Concerns about Extremism, Continuing Discontent with U.S.* (Washington, DC: Pew Research Center, 2009).

53 "Ahl-e-Sunnat Parties to Launch Movement against Talibanisation," *Daily Times,* May 7, 2009.

54 Steve Breyman and Aneel Salman, "Reaping the Whirlwind: Pakistani Counterinsurgency," *Fletcher Forum of World Affairs* 34, no. 2 (2010): 72.

55 Syed Manzar Abbad Zaidi, "The United States and the Counterinsurgency: The Peace Process in Pakistan," *American Foreign Policy Interests* 31, no. 3 (May 2009): 153.

56 Zaidi, " United States and the Counterinsurgency," 154.

57 Iqbal Khattak, "Bajaur Operation 25 to 35% Intense," *Daily Times,* September 2, 2008.

58 Rahman Ullah, "The Battle for Pakistan: Militancy and Conflict in Bajaur," (Washington, DC: New American Foundation, 2010), 8.

59 Zaidi, "United States and the Counterinsurgency," 153.

60 Galula, *Counterinsurgency Warfare,* 55.

61 Rahimullah Yusufzai, "Assessing the Progress of Pakistan's South Waziristan Offensive," *CTC Sentinel* 2, no. 12 (2009): 8–12.

62 C. Christine Fair and Seth G. Jones, *Counterinsurgency in Pakistan* (Santa Monica, CA: Rand Corporation, 2010), 74.

63 "PM Sharif Announces another Push for Taliban Peace Talks," *Dawn,* January 29, 2014.

64 "TTP Claims Attack on Karachi Airport," *Dawn*, June 8, 2014.
65 Ismail Khan, "All-Out Military Operation Launched in North Waziristan," *Dawn*, June 16, 2014.
66 Syed Irfan Raza, "Zarb-i-Azb Is War of Survival, Says ISPR Chief," *Dawn*, June 27, 2014.
67 Farrukh Saleem, "Winning Ground War, Losing 500,000 Hearts and Minds," *The News*, June 27, 2014.
68 Paul Melshen, "Mapping out a Counterinsurgency Campaign Plan: Critical Considerations in Counterinsurgency Campaigning," *Small Wars & Insurgencies* 18, no.4 (2007): 681.
69 John A. Nagl, *Learning to Eat Soup with a Knife: Counterinsurgency Lessons from Malaya and Vietnam* (Chicago, IL: University of Chicago Press, 2005), xxi–xxv.
70 Melshen, "Mapping out a Counterinsurgency Campaign Plan," 681.
71 Cited in Ucko and Egnell, *Counterinsurgency in Crisis,* 10.
72 Andrew Mumford, *The Counter-Insurgency Myth: The British Experience of Irregular Warfare* (New York: Routledge, 2012), 5.
73 Eliot A. Cohen, "Constraints on America's Conduct of Small Wars," *International Security* 9, no. 2 (1984): 167.
74 Seth G. Jones, *Counterinsurgency in Afghanistan* (Santa Monica, CA: Rand Corporation, 2008): 10, 16.
75 Mullick, *Helping Pakistan Defeat the Taliban,* 20.
76 Athar Abbas interview.
77 Shuja Nawaz, "Learning by Doing: The Pakistan Army's Experience with Counterinsurgency," *Atlantic Council* (2011): 9.
78 Yochi J. Drezen and Siobahn Gorbman, "U.S. Special Forces Sent to Train Pakistan," *Wall Street Journal,* May 16, 2009.
79 As of November 2008, the training was limited to the select senior Frontier Corpsmen, who would impart the training to the rest of the force. Jason H. Campbell and Jeremy Shapiro, *Brookings' Afghanistan Index: Tracking Progress and Security in Post-9/11 Afghanistan* (Brookings Institution, Washington, DC, 2009), 34.
80 Michael D. Maples, "Annual Threat Assessment: Statement before the Committee on Armed Services, United States Senate," February 2008: 22; Michael D. Maples, "Annual Threat Assessment: Statement before the Committee on Armed Services, United States Senate," March 2009, 12.
81 Stephen P. Cohen and Shuja Nawaz, *Mastering Counterinsurgency: A Workshop Report* (Brookings Counterinsurgency and Pakistan Paper Series, July 7, 2009).
82 Mullick, *Helping Pakistan Defeat the Taliban,* 21.
83 Mullick, *Helping Pakistan Defeat the Taliban,* 19.
84 Sameer Lalwani, "Pakistan's COIN Flip: The Recent History of Pakistani Military Counterinsurgency Operations in the NWFP and FATA," Counter-insurgency Strategy Initiative Policy Paper, 2010: 6.
85 Sameer Lalwani, "The Pakistan Military's Adaptation to Counterinsurgency in 2009," *CTC Sentinel* 3, no. 1 (2010): 10.
86 Lalwani, "Pakistan Military," 10.
87 Mumford, *Counter-Insurgency Myth,* 6.
88 Rod Thornton, "The British Army and the Origins of Its Minimum Force Philosophy," *Small Wars and Insurgencies* 15, no.1 (2004): 84.
89 John Lynn, "Patterns of Insurgency and Counterinsurgency," *Military Review* (2005): 27.
90 Samarjit Ghosh, "Insurgency in the FATA & NWFP: Challenges and Prospects for the Pakistan Army," *Manekshaw Paper no. 6* (2008): 18.
91 Dixon, "Hearts and Minds?": 353.

92   Mullick, *Helping Pakistan Defeat the Taliban,* 6.
93   Mullick, *Helping Pakistan Defeat the Taliban,* 14.
94   Brain Cloughley, "Insurrection, Terrorism and the Pakistan Army," Pakistan's Security Research Unit, Brief No. 53 (2009): 17.
95   Athar Abbas interview.
96   Fair and Jones, *Counterinsurgency in Pakistan*: 71.
97   Interview with a military brigadier, in Kharian, Punjab, Pakistan, June 24, 2014. He fought insurgents in South Waziristan, and he preferred to remain anonymous.
98   Syed Adnan Ali Shah Bukhari, "New Strategies in Pakistan's Counter-Insurgency Operation in South Waziristan," *Terrorism Monitor* 7, no. 37 (2009): 1–12.
99   Iftikhar A. Khan, "Kayani Writes to Mehsuds, Seek Tribe's Support," *Dawn,* October 20, 2009.
100 Lalwani, "Pakistan Military's Adaptation": 12.
101 Breyman and Salman, "Reaping the Whirlwind": 76.
102 Pamela Constable, "Pakistan Treads Lightly as New Fight Looms," *Washington Post,* June 29, 2009.
103 Talat Masood, "Military Operation in North Waziristan: An Overview," *Express Tribune,* June 25, 2014.
104 Melshen, "Mapping Out": 671.
105 Timothy K. Deady, "Lessons from a Successful Counterinsurgency: The Philippines 1899–1902," *Parameters* 35, no. 1 (2005): 58.
106 James M. Dubik, *Operational Air in Counterinsurgency: A View from the Inside* (Washington, DC: Institute for the Study of War, 2012), 16.
107 Dubik, *Operational Air in Counterinsurgency,* 17.
108 Anthony Lloyd, "Captured Battle Plan Shows Strength and Training of Taleban Forces," *The Times* (London), November 11, 2008.
109 "Forces Regain Control of Bajaur," *The News,* March 3, 2010.
110 "Street Battles Rage in Uzbek Militants' Stronghold," *Dawn,* November 2, 2009.
111 Zahid Hussain, "Laddah, Sararogha Cleared; Street Fighting in Makin," *Dawn,* November 18, 2009.
112 "Five More Militants Killed in South Waziristan: ISPR," *Dawn,* December 10, 2009.
113 "Army Breaks Myth about SWA," *The Nation,* November 18, 2009.
114 "Arms Recovered from Terrorists Enough for 15-Year War," *The News,* November 16, 2014.
115 "Editorial: Military Operation," *Dawn,* June 9, 2015.
116 "Grading Zarb-E-Azb; One Year and Counting," *Pakistan Today,* June 14, 2015.
117 Mullick, *Helping Pakistan Defeat the Taliban,* 21.
118 "Terrorists Thrown Out from Fata for Good: Army Chief," *Dawn,* September 17, 2015.
119 Rahimullah Yusufzai, "Zarb-E-Azb: Findings and Conclusions," *The News,* June 21, 2015.
120 Galula, *Counterinsurgency Warfare*: 63.
121 Dixon, "Hearts and Minds?": 362.
122 Robert Grainger Ker Thompson, *Defeating Communist Insurgency: The Lessons of Malaya and Vietnam* (New York: Frederick A. Praeger, 1966), 112–13, 161.
123 Michael Fitzsimmons, "Hard Hearts and Open Minds? Governance, Identity and the Intellectual Foundations of Counterinsurgency Strategy," *Journal of Strategic Studies* 31, no. 3 (2008): 341.
124 *Counterinsurgency,* US Army Field Manual 3-24, December 2006, accessed July 25, 2015, http://usacac.army.mil/cac2/Repository/Materials/COIN-FM3-24.pdf.

125 "FATA Sustainable Development Plan 2007–2015," Civil Secretariat FATA, Peshawar, n.d.: 11.
126 Krista Mahr, "Million Displaced Pakistanis Face Tough Choices before Going Home," *Reuters*, March 16, 2016.
127 Interview with a military brigadier, in Kharian, Punjab, Pakistan, October 10, 2013. He commanded the forces fighting the insurgents. He requested anonymity.
128 "FATA Temporarily Displaced Persons Emergency Recovery Project," Report No. PAD2141, *World Bank*, August 30, 2017: 9–10.
129 "Final Phase of South Waziristan IDPs' Return Begins on Tuesday," *Dawn*, July 23, 2017.
130 "The Government of Pakistan Launches the FATA Sustainable Return and Rehabilitation Strategy," UN Development Programme, April 7, 2015, accessed on December 12, 2015, http://www.pk.undp.org/content/pakistan/en/home/p resscenter/pressreleases/2015/04/07/the-government-of-pakistan-launches-the-fat a-sustainable-return.
131 Jon Boone and Emma Graham, "Pakistan Unprepared for Refugees Fleeing Operation against Taliban," *The Guardian*, June 26, 2014.
132 Hiba Mahamadi, "Interview: Hassan, Internally Displaced Person from Ladha, South Waziristan," *Newsline*, December 2014.
133 "FATA Secretariat Receives Rs 5 Billion for Repatriation and Rehabilitation of IDPs," *Pakistan Today*, August 30, 2015.
134 Interview, Khan Zaib Burki, Islamabad, March 21, 2019. He is based in Islamabad but he frequently visits his home town in the South Waziristan Agency of FATA.
135 Saad Sayeed and Radha Shah, "Displacement, Repatriation and Rehabilitation: Stories of Dispossession from Pakistan's Frontier," Working Paper FG8, Stiftung Wissenschaft und Politik, Berlin, April 2017: 7.
136 Shahzaib Khan, "FATA's Belated Decolonization," *Express Tribune*, June 3, 2018.
137 Shaukat Qadir, "State's Responses to the Pakistani Taliban Onslaught," in *Insurgency and Counterinsurgent in South Asia: Through A Peace Building lens,* ed. Moeed Yusuf (Washington, DC: United States Institute of Peace, 2014), 154.
138 Farhan Zahid, "The Success and Failures of Pakistan's Operation Zarb-E-Azb," *Terrorism Monitor* 13, no. 14 (2015): 5.
139 "Pakistani Taliban Splits; New Faction by the Name of 'TTP Jamatul Ahrar' Comes into Existence," *Economic Times*, August 26, 2014.
140 Zahir Shah Sherazi, "Six Top TTP Commanders Announce Allegiance to Islamic State's Baghdadi," *Dawn*, October 14, 2014.
141 Zahid, "Success and Failures," 6.
142 Dean Nelson, Taha Siddiqui, and Ashfaq Yusufzai, "Mullah Radio, Terrorist Demagogue behind the Savagery of Peshawar," *The Telegraph*, December 20, 2014.
143 Zahid, "Success and Failures": 6.
144 Declan Walsh, Ihsanullah Tipu Mehsud, and Ismail Khan, "Taliban Attack at Bacha Khan University in Pakistan Renews Fears," *New York Times*, January 20, 2016.
145 Farhan Zahid, "The Pakistani Taliban after the Peshawar School Attack," *Terrorism Monitor* 13, no. 1 (2015): 3.

Bibliography

Abbas, Hassan. "A Profile of Tehrik-i-Taliban Pakistan." *CTC Sentinel* 1, no.2 (January2008): 1–3.

Ahmad, Ishtiaq. "The U.S. Af-Pak Strategy: Challenges and Opportunities for Pakistan." *Asian Affairs: An American Review* 37, no. 4 (2010): 191–209.

"Ahl-e-Sunnat Parties to Launch Movement against Talibanisation." *Daily Times*, May 7, 2009.

Akhtar, Shahzad. "Decline of Insurgency in Pakistan's FATA: A Counterinsurgency Perspective." *Asian Survey* 54, no. 4 (2019): 693–716.

Ali, Imtiaz. "Military Victory in South Waziristan or the Beginning of a Long War." *Terrorism Monitor* 38, no. 202 (2009): 1–10.

Armitage, Richard L., Samuel R. Berger, and Daniel S. Markey. *U.S. Strategy for Pakistan and Afghanistan (Independent Task Force Report No. 65)*. New York and Washington, DC: Council on Foreign Relations, 2010.

"Arms Recovered from Terrorists Enough for 15-Year War." *The News*, November 16, 2014.

"Army Breaks Myth about SWA." *The Nation*, November 18, 2009.

Aslam, M.W. "Understanding the 'Pak' in 'AfPak': The Obama Administration's Security Policy for Pakistan at the Mid-Term." *Journal of Policing, Intelligence and Counter Terrorism* 7, no. 1 (2012): 2–21.

Bergen, Peter, and Katherine Tiedemann. *Revenge of the Drones: An Analysis of Drone Strikes in Pakistan*. Washington, DC: New America Foundation, 2009.

Bergen, Peter, and Katherine Tiedemann. "Washington's Phantom War: The Effects of the U.S. Drone Program in Pakistan." *Foreign Affairs* 90, no. 4 (2011): 12–18.

Boone, Jon, and Emma Graham. "Pakistan Unprepared for Refugees Fleeing Operation against Taliban." *The Guardian*, June 26, 2014.

Breyman, Steve, and Aneel Salman. "Reaping the Whirlwind: Pakistani Counterinsurgency." *Fletcher Forum of World Affairs* 34, no. 2 (2010): 65–85.

Bukhari, Syed Adnan Ali Shah. "New Strategies in Pakistan's Counter-Insurgency Operation in South Waziristan." *Terrorism Monitor* 7, no. 37 (2009): 1–12.

Campbell, Jason H. and Jeremy Shapiro. *Brookings' Afghanistan Index: Tracking Progress and Security in Post-9/11 Afghanistan*. Washington, DC: Brookings Institution, 2009.

Cloughley, Brain. "Insurrection, Terrorism and the Pakistan Army." Pakistan's Security Research Unit, Brief no. 53, 2009.

Cohen, Eliot A. "Constraints on America's Conduct of Small Wars." *International Security* 9, no. 2 (1984): 151–181.

Cohen, Stephen P. and Shuja Nawaz. *Mastering Counterinsurgency: A Workshop Report*. Brookings Counterinsurgency and Pakistan Paper Series, July 7, 2009.

Constable, Pamela. "Pakistan Treads Lightly as New Fight Looms." *Washington Post*, June 29, 2009.

Council on Foreign Relations. "Obama's Strategy for Afghanistan and Pakistan, March 2009." *Council on Foreign Relations*, 2009. Accessed August 31, 2016, http://www.cfr.org/pakistan/obamas-strategy-afghanistan-pakistan-march-2009/p18952.

Deady, Timothy K. "Lessons from a Successful Counterinsurgency: The Philippines 1899–1902." *Parameters* 35, no. 1 (2005): 53–58.

De Young, Karen. "U.S. Offers New Role for Pakistan: A Broader Partnership." *The Washington Post*, November 30, 2009.

Dixon, Paul. "Hearts and Minds? British Counterinsurgency from Malay to Iraq." *Journal of Strategic Studies* 32, no. 3 (2009): 353–381.

Drezen, Yochi J. and Siobahn Gorbman, "U.S. Special Forces Sent to Train Pakistan." *Wall Street Journal*, May 16, 2009.

Dubik, James M. *Operational Air in Counterinsurgency: A View from the Inside.* Washington, DC: Institute for the Study of War, 2012.

"Editorial: Military Operation." *Dawn*, June 9, 2015.

Fair, C. Christine. "Time for Sober Realism: Renegotiating U.S. Relations with Pakistan." *The Washington Quarterly* 32, no. 2 (2009): 149–172.

Fair, Christine C., and Seth G. Jones. *Counterinsurgency in Pakistan.* Santa Monica, CA: Rand Corporation, 2010.

"FATA Secretariat Receives Rs 5 Billion for Repatriation and Rehabilitation of IDPs." *Pakistan Today*, August 30, 2015.

"FATA Sustainable Development Plan 2007–2015." Peshawar: Civil Secretariat FATA, n.d.

"FATA Temporarily Displaced Persons Emergency Recovery Project." Report No. PAD2141. World Bank, August 30, 2017.

"Final Phase of South Waziristan IDPs' Return Begins on Tuesday." *Dawn*, July 23, 2017.

Fitzsimmons, Michael. "Hard Hearts and Open Minds? Governance, Identity and the Intellectual Foundations of Counterinsurgency Strategy." *Journal of Strategic Studies* 31, no. 3 (2008): 337–365.

"Five More Militants Killed in South Waziristan: ISPR." *Dawn*, December 10, 2009.

"Forces Regain Control of Bajaur." *The News*, March 3, 2010.

Galula, David. *Counterinsurgency Warfare: Theory and Practice.* Westport, CT: Praeger Security International, 2006.

Ghosh, Samarjit. "Insurgency in the FATA & NWFP: Challenges and Prospects for the Pakistan Army." *Manekshaw Paper no. 6* (2008): 18.

"Grading Zarb-E-Azb; One Year and Counting." *Pakistan Today*, June 14, 2015.

Grainger Ker Thompson, Robert. *Defeating Communist Insurgency: The Lessons of Malaya and Vietnam.* New York: Frederick A. Praeger, 1966.

Irfan Raza, Syed. "Zarb-i-Azb Is War of Survival, Says ISPR Chief." *Dawn*, June 27, 2014.

Jones, Seth G. *Counterinsurgency in Afghanistan.* Santa Monica, CA: Rand Corporation, 2008.

Joyner, James. "Obama Orders Pakistan Drone Attacks." *Atlantic Council*, January 24, 2009.

Kfir, Isaac. "U.S. Policy Toward Pakistan and Afghanistan under the Obama Administration." *The Middle East Review of International Affairs* 13, no. 4 (December2009): 20–33.

Khan, Iftikhar A. "Kayani Writes to Mehsuds, Seek Tribe's Support." *Dawn*, October 20, 2009.

Khan, Ismail. "All-Out Military Operation Launched in North Waziristan." *Dawn*, June 16, 2014.

Khan, Mukhtar A. "Pakistani Government Offensive in Swat Heading for the Taliban of Waziristan." *Terrorism Monitor* 7, no. 17 (June2009).

Khan, Shahzaib. "FATA's Belated Decolonization." *Express Tribune*, June 3, 2018.

Khattak, Iqbal. "Bajaur Operation 25 to 35% Intense." *Daily Times*, September 2, 2008.

Koelbl, Susanne. "Pakistan's New Intelligence Chief: Terror Is Our Enemy, Not India." *Der Spiegel*, January 6, 2009.

Kronstadt, K. Alan. *Pakistan–US Relations*. Congressional Research Service, *Report No. RL33498*, 2009.

Kronstadt, K. Alan. *Pakistan: Key Current Issues and Developments*. Congressional Research Service, *Report No. R41307*, 2010. Accessed on June 17, 2016, https://www.fas.org/sgp/crs/row/R41307.pdf.

Lalwani, Sameer. "Pakistan's COIN Flip: The Recent History of Pakistani Military Counterinsurgency Operations in the NWFP and FATA." *Counterinsurgency Strategy Initiative Policy Paper*, 2010.

Lalwani, Sameer. "The Pakistan Military's Adaptation to Counterinsurgency in 2009." *CTC Sentinel* 3, no. 1 (2010): 9–13.

Lloyd, Anthony. "Captured Battle Plan Shows Strength and Training of Taleban Forces." *The Times* (London), November 11, 2008.

Lynn, John. "Patterns of Insurgency and Counterinsurgency." *Military Review* (2005): 22–27.

Mahamadi, Hiba. "Interview: Hassan, Internally Displaced Person from Ladha, South Waziristan." *Newsline*, December2014.

Mahr, Krista. "Million Displaced Pakistanis Face Tough Choices before Going Home." *Reuters*, March 16, 2016.

Mahsud, Ishtiaq. "Desperation in Pakistani Hospitals, Refugee Camps." *Associated Press*, May 9, 2009.

Maples, Michael D. *"Annual Threat Assessment: Statement before the Committee on Armed Services"*. United States Senate, February 2008.

Maples, Michael D. *"Annual Threat Assessment: Statement before the Committee on Armed Services."* United States Senate, March 2009.

Markey, Daniel. *From AfPak to PakAf: A Response to the New US Strategy for South Asia*. Washington DC: Council on Foreign Relations, 2009.

Masood, Talat. "Military Operation in North Waziristan: An Overview." *Express Tribune*, June 25, 2014.

Melshen, Paul. "Mapping out a Counterinsurgency Campaign Plan: Critical Considerations in Counterinsurgency Campaigning." *Small Wars & Insurgencies* 18, no. 4 (2007): 665–698.

Miller, Paul D. "How to Exercise U.S. Leverage Over Pakistan." *The Washington Quarterly* 35, no. 4 (2012): 37–52.

Mullick, Haider Ali Hussin. *Helping Pakistan Defeat the Taliban: A Joint Action Agenda for the United States and Pakistan*. Institute for Social Policy and Understanding, 2009.

Mumford, Andrew. *The Counter-Insurgency Myth: The British Experience of Irregular Warfare*. New York: Routledge, 2012.

Nagl, John A. *Learning to Eat Soup with a Knife: Counterinsurgency Lessons from Malaya and Vietnam*. Chicago, IL: University of Chicago Press, 2005.

Nawaz, Shuja. "Learning by Doing: The Pakistan Army's Experience with Counterinsurgency." *Atlantic Council*, 2011.

Nelson, Dean, Taha Siddiqui, and Ashfaq Yusufzai. "Mullah Radio, Terrorist Demagogue behind the Savagery of Peshawar." *The Telegraph*, December 20, 2014.

New America Foundation. *The Year of the Drone: An Analysis of US Drone Strikes in Pakistan, 2004–2011*. Washington DC: New America Foundation, 2011.

"PAF Ready to Thwart Indian Designs: Air Chief." *The News*, March 28, 2010.

"Pak to Get 18 F-16s, Shadow Drones Likely Within a Year." *The Indian Express*, March 30, 2010.

"Pakistani Taliban Splits; New Faction by the Name of 'TTP Jamatul Ahrar' Comes into Existence." *Economic Times*, August 26, 2014.

Parsons, Paul Richter, and Christi Parsons. "Obama Prepares to Meet with Leaders of Afghanistan, Pakistan." *Los Angeles Times*, May 5, 2009.

Pew Global Attitudes Project. *Pakistani Public Opinion: Growing Concerns about Extremism, Continuing Discontent with U.S.* Washington, DC: Pew Research Center, 2009.

"PM Sharif Announces another Push for Taliban Peace Talks." *Dawn*, January 29, 2014.

Qadir, Shaukat. "State's Responses to the Pakistani Taliban Onslaught." In *Insurgency and Counterinsurgent in South Asia: Through A Peace Building lens*, edited by Moeed Yusuf. Washington, DC: United States Institute of Peace, 2014.

Ramsay, Clay, Steven Kull, Stephen Weber, and Evan Lewis. *Pakistani Public Opinion on the Swat Conflict, Afghanistan, and the US*. Washington, DC: The University of Maryland, 2009.

Rashid, Ahmed. "Pakistan's Continued Failure to Adopt a Counterinsurgency Strategy." *CTC Sentinel* 2, no. 3 (March 2009).

Saleem, Farrukh. "Winning Ground War, Losing 500,000 Hearts and Mind." *The News*, June 27, 2014.

Sayeed, Saad, and Radha Shah. "Displacement, Repatriation and Rehabilitation: Stories of Dispossession from Pakistan's Frontier," Working Paper FG8. Berlin: Stiftung Wissenschaft und Politik, April 2017.

Sherazi, Zahir Shah. "Six Top TTP Commanders Announce Allegiance to Islamic State's Baghdadi." *Dawn*, October 14, 2014.

Smith, M. L. R. "A Tradition That Never Was: Critiquing the Critique of British COIN." *Small Wars Journal* (2012).

"Street Battles Rage in Uzbek Militants' Stronghold." *Dawn*, November 2, 2009.

"Terrorists Thrown Out from Fata for Good: Army Chief." *Dawn*, September 17, 2015.

"The Government of Pakistan Launches the FATA Sustainable Return and Rehabilitation Strategy." UN Development Programme, April 7, 2015.

Thornton, Rod. "The British Army and the Origins of Its Minimum Force Philosophy." *Small Wars and Insurgencies* 15, no. 1 (2004): 88–106.

"TTP Claims Attack on Karachi Airport." *Dawn*, June 8, 2014.

Ucko, David H. and Robert Egnell. *Counterinsurgency in Crisis: Britain and the Challenges of Modern Warfare*. New York: Colombia University Press, 2013.

Ullah, Rahman. "The Battle for Pakistan: Militancy and Conflict in Bajaur." Washington, DC: New American Foundation, 2010.

"US Delivers Cobra Gunships to Pakistan." *Nation*, March 17, 2010.

Walsh, Declan, Ihsanullah Tipu Mehsud, and Ismail Khan, "Taliban Attack at Bacha Khan University in Pakistan Renews Fears." *New York Times*, January 20, 2016.

White House. "White Paper of the Interagency Policy Group's Report on US Policy towards Afghanistan and Pakistan." Washington, DC, March 2009. Accessed on March 15, 2016, https://www.whitehouse.gov/assets/documents/Afghanistan-Pakistan_White_Paper.pdf.

Yusufzai, Rahimullah. "Assessing the Progress of Pakistan's South Waziristan Offensive." *CTC Sentinel* 2, no. 12 (2009): 8–12.

Yusufzai, Rahimullah. "Zarb-E-Azb: Findings and Conclusions." *The News*, June 21, 2015.

Zahid, Farhan. "The Pakistani Taliban after the Peshawar School Attack." *Terrorism Monitor* 13, no. 1 (2015): 3–5.

Zahid, Farhan. "The Success and Failures of Pakistan's Operation Zarb-E-Azb." *Terrorism Monitor* 13, no. 14 (2015): 1–3.

Zahid, Gishkori, "Pakistan Receives Three New F-16s." *Express Tribune*, June 27, 2010.

Zahid, Hussain, "Laddah, Sararogha Cleared; Street Fighting in Makin," *Dawn*, November 18, 2009.

Zaidi, Syed Manzar Abbad. "The United States and the Counterinsurgency: The Peace Process in Pakistan." *American Foreign Policy Interests* 31, no. 3 (May 2009): 149, 165.

5   Aftereffects of Insurgency in FATA

Integration of the FATA, Rise of PTM and Resurgence of the TTP

This chapter discusses how the FATA (Federally Administered Tribal Areas) has transformed over the last two decades of insurgency and counter-insurgency operations. This chapter features the most important development that has taken place so far is the integration of the FATA region into the neighboring province of Khyber Pakhtunkhwa (KPK) with the aim of bringing socioeconomic and political development. The semi-autonomous status of FATA and the resulting socioeconomic and political under-development has long been considered as one of the main factors responsible for increased militancy. However, FATA merger with KPK through a con-stitutional amendment is not well-supported with the necessary legal, administrative, and financial measures to facilitate and complete the process of integration. Therefore, there is rising public anger over the slow pace of development in the region. This chapter further focuses on the rise and growing popularity of the Pashtun Tahafaz Movement (PTM) which is evi-dent from the mounting public frustrations. The PTM has emerged as a nonviolent social movement to protect the rights of the FATA people. This chapter also discusses resurgence of the Tehrik-e-Taliban Pakistan (TTP) as an organization under its current leader Nur Wali Mehsud who has infused new vigor in the organization by bringing the breakaway factions together and improving internal discipline. The TTP's acceleration of terrorist attacks with the recent rise of the Afghan Taliban in Afghanistan after the with-drawal of the American forces and the Pakistani government's attempts to engage the TTP in talks has also been discussed.

Integration of FATA with KPK

There was recognition among the policy making circles that much of the problem of terrorism and insurgency in FATA could be attributed to its semi-autonomous status and the weak writ of the Pakistani state.[1] Almost all political parties developed a consensus over the integration of FATA into the mainstream Pakistani state which envisioned the elimination of the grie-vances of the people.[2] The idea of FATA reforms was first conceived when the Pakistani government devised the National Action Plan to eradicate

DOI: 10.4324/9781003349259-5

terrorism in the aftermath of the most horrific attack on Peshawar Army Public School in December 2014 that killed 140 children. In November 2015, the then-prime minister Nawaz Sharif set up a committee on FATA reforms which suggested in its August 2016 report the merger of FATA with the adjacent province, Khyber Pakhtunkhwa, in "a gradual and phased approach", and repealing the Frontier Crimes Regulations.[3] To implement these proposals, the parliament of Pakistan on May 28, 2018 passed the Twenty-fifth Amendment to the Constitution of Pakistan that ended the semiautonomous status of the former FATA and merged it with the province of Khyber Pakhtunkhwa and repealed Article 247 of the constitution.[4]

The revoking of the Article 247 enabled parliament to legislate for FATA and extended the jurisdiction of the higher judiciary to the tribal areas.[5] Thus, the merger has paved the way for the approximately five million residents of the FATA to enjoy their constitutional rights. The merger of FATA through the 31st amendment marked as a watershed moment in the history of the region. In the words of one major daily newspaper's editorial: "History has been made. FATA is no more ... the people of the region now have formal access to the constitutional and political rights that are legally available to all citizens of Pakistan."[6]

Following the constitutional amendment regarding the merger, the extension of the formal judicial system to the integrated areas, now called (the Newly Merged Districts, or NMDs), started in March 2019 but it has been faced with numerous challenges. The government initially planned to implement reforms in a gradual manner that is to introduce government institutions in a phased fashion. During the first phase, the plan envisioned the provision of basic services such as education, health, and road infrastructure. Further, the introduction and implementation of the formal criminal justice system would take place over a period of five years as the government required time to build the necessary infrastructure and to develop the human resources.

During this transition period, the government introduced the FATA interim Governance Regulations (2018) to serve as a legal framework. However, the Peshawar High Court declared the interim regulations in violation of the constitution.[7] The Supreme Court in a January 2019 ruling reiterated that former FATA areas have become part of Khyber Pakhtunkhwa and the people of the newly formed districts must be treated according to the law of land. The Supreme Court ordered the government of Khyber Pakhtunkhwa to build the necessary infrastructure within six months to establish a uniform court system in the newly integrated areas. The Supreme Court's ruling posed serious challenges to the provincial government in terms of developing the infrastructure and capacity within such a short span of time.

In terms of socio-economic development, the FATA region lags far behind from the other parts of the country. The reasons for lacking political and socioeconomic development can be found in the long-held semiautonomous status of the region and neglect of the successive governments in Pakistan from 1947. The region's socioeconomic development deteriorated further over the nearly two decades of insurgency and counterinsurgency operations. At present, the region stands as one of the poorest regions of Pakistan, offering little in terms of public services such as health care, education, and employment. Majority of the population of the FATA have been suffering from abject poverty. Reportedly, two-thirds of the FATA's overall population live in poverty.[8] A UN report affirms that the FATA ranks lowest among Pakistan's eighteen regions in terms of human development indicators.[9]

Apart from serious issues related with socio-economic development of the region, there are reports of widespread human rights violations as the people are sandwiched in the fight between the militant groups and the Pakistani security forces.[10] The conflict related sufferings has only aggravated the frustrations of the local people of FATA. Moreover, the local communities are unhappy with the permanent deployment of military troops in FATA after breaking the insurgents' hold, especially given military mistreatment that often-involved frequent inspections and harsh attitude of soldiers with the civilian population at the security checkposts established every few kilometers. These checkposts were manned by soldiers from other parts of the country with little knowledge of local Pashtun culture or its traditions. Body searches of the locals by the soldiers amounted to the violation of local traditions which created further resentment.[11]

The grievances of the local communities, particularly in South and North Waziristan Agencies are serious. They complained that their houses and businesses were destroyed during the military operations and were not rebuilt.[12] Although, the FATA has been merged into the neighboring KPK through a constitutional amendment, but practical steps regarding legal, administrative, and financial matters to facilitate integration are not forthcoming which has only generated public frustrations.[13] The emergence of the Pashtun Tahafuz Movement (PTM), a new civil movement of FATA Pashtuns, demonstrates local communities' discontentment with the government's policies. The PTM has demanded the constitutional rights of the Pashtuns living in FATA and beyond, which has attracted many alienated people of the FATA. The PTM has also launched peaceful protests demanding the return of the dislocated population to their home places, an end to extrajudicial killings and disappearances, and clearance of land mines in FATA.[14] The following section details how the growing frustrations of the public led to the birth of the PTM which has unequivocally demanded an end to the presence of military troops in the tribal districts along with provision of basic rights to the FATA people.

Rise of Pashtun Tahafaz Movement (PTM)

The rise of the Pashtun Tahafuz Movement, a non-violent protest movement, can be attributed to the public impatience and frustration that resulted from the slow process of introducing governance and the permanent deployment of the military troops in the region. The genesis of PTM can be traced back to the protests launched against the extrajudicial murder of Naqeebullah Mehsud, a young Pashtun hailed from the tribal areas. Naqeebullah who was living in Karachi since 2008 was killed by the Counter Terrorism Department (CTD) on dubious charges of terrorism. In a 10-day sit-in in Islamabad in February 2018, the Pashtuns activists not only demanded justice for Mehsud but also recorded their protests over the Pakistani military's policies in the erstwhile FATA. The protestants also demanded basic human rights for the tribal people and release of "missing persons" who were arrested or detained by the security forces during military operations in the tribal areas.[15] This protest developed into social movement which later named as Pashtun Tahafuz Movement, and Manzoor Pashteen was appointed its leader.

The PTM launched a protest campaign that targeted the extrajudicial killings by security forces and building of checkposts in the region. To them, these posts have unnecessarily curtailed the movement of people. In addition, the PTM has outrightly rejected the state's policies of the last two decades that they believed inflicted miseries on ordinary Pashtuns. They blamed both the Taliban and the security forces behind the destruction and sufferings of the FATA people.[16] Despite its ethnonationalist origin and its campaign to promote Pashtun nationalism, PTM has mainly stood for human rights and rule of law. One of the main PTM leader echoes this: "We have created a golden opportunity for Islamabad to shun its past as a security state and function as a normal country concerned with the welfare of its citizens."[17] Nasar argues that the bitter experience of imposed war provided courage, strength, tolerance, and a sense of struggle to highlight Pashtuns' sufferings in the state of Pakistan.[18] Apart from challenging the military presence and its policies in the FATA, the PTM has challenged the forces such as 'tribal' elders that favor *status quo* in the tribal region.[19] A movement of mostly young Pashtun has also challenged the decades-old patriarchal values of the region.[20] Women have actively participated in the PTM to fight for the Pashtun cause in Pakistan.[21]

The leadership has categorically declared that the PTM would never use violence to achieve its objectives. In a rally organized by the movement, the leaders of the PTM maintained, "All our demands and activities are in accordance with the philosophy on non-violence. We have so far not disturbed the lives and occupations of ordinary citizens during all our previous rallies."[22] The PTM has invoked the country constitution to draft its demands. Ali Wazir, a founding leader of the PTM said that the PTM "wants the state to recognize us as equal citizens and grant us everything that goes with that."[23] Because of the legitimate demands and the nonviolent nature of the movement, the PTM has gained widespread popularity among Pashtun community despite Pakistani military establishment serious opposition.[24] A significant section of the civil society in Pakistan beyond the Pashtuns community has endorsed the PTM goals.[25]

The PTM is not well received in the circles of the Pakistani establishment, especially the military. The PTM leadership has been criticized for giving antimilitary statements that could potentially discredit the Pakistani army.[26] Some of the PTM's slogans especially targeting the Pakistan Army have enraged the military leadership establishment and PTM was presented as a threat. Therefore, the PTM is accused of being funded and supported by "foreign" powers, who want to destabilize Pakistan.[27] Chief of the Army Staff, General Bajwa labelled the PTM a "suspicious movement."[28] The military's spokesperson also raised the question of the popularity of PTM in Afghanistan and said it "was problematic," which was an attempt to create doubts over the motives of the PTM.[29] Some of the PTM leaders have made their way into the parliament through election, yet they have been portrayed by the military establishment as 'Indian agents' or 'enemies of the state.'[30]

Some voices have criticized over the military's dubbing of PTM leadership as traitors, because PTM which is a nonviolent movement has provided a platform to air the legitimate public grievances that could in turn prevent people from joining the extremist or violent groups. Critical of the Pakistani government approach towards the PTM, Hassan Abbas, contends, "PTM should have been welcomed by Islamabad as an ally against the extremist and radical ideologies propagated in the tribal areas, but short-sightedness served as an obstacle to such an understanding."[31] The Pakistani military has enlisted the help of extremist elements to oppose the PTM. A retired military officer organized an anti-PTM rally in April 2018, under the banner of Pakistan Zindabad (Long Live Pakistan) Movement and identified the PTM members "foreign agents."[32] Ali Wazir, an elected member of Pakistan's National Assembly and leader of the movement, explained, "It is ironic that the institutions responsible for protecting Pakistan's territorial integrity and protecting it from dangerous threats are bankrolling thugs to launch a Pakistan Zindabad Movement. ... It is telling that former Taliban commanders have addressed their gatherings. We also have indications that efforts are underway to mobilize sectarian terrorists and other fanatics to 'counter' our peaceful campaign."[33]

It is believed that PTM narrative developed some resonance with the power circles which forced the state and the military to "expedite" the FATA reforms process, abolishing the FCR and allowing for FATA's integration into mainstream Pakistan.[34] In addition, many young tribal Pashtuns get exposure and awareness of their rights, while living in the urban cities during the conflict, and are demanding from the state facilities such as access to the basic health and education facilities. PTM has served as a vehicle to get their voices heard.[35] However, supporters and followers of PTM continued to face repression from state in the form of arrests, kidnapping and coercion.[36] The use of repressions tends to alienate the people which in turn can be translated into support for the violent movements. In addition, a combination of a pervasive perception of injustice and suppression of any nonviolent protest movements could seriously intensify local grievances that could be tapped by the TTP. In addition, the State agencies increased monitoring and involvement with PTM activists could risk their attention away from TTP ideology and activities, thus helping the latter to grow.

Instead of repressing the people or peaceful protest, the government needs to provide transparent channels to voice their legitimate grievances. The government should also launch socioeconomic development projects and build the capacity of law enforcement agencies with special emphasis on the rule of law, the delivery of justice, and the provision of essential public goods to reinforce human security along with providing employment, education, and healthcare. A failure to address these issues on the part of the government could possibly intensify public grievances which TTP would be ready to tap. Some analysts warned that TTP has garnered some public support in view of the prevailing grievances. Hassan Abbas maintained that TTP's revival in recent years can be attributed to Pakistani government half-heated measures to bring the much-needed socio-economic development and rule of law as proposed in the 2018 FATA Reforms Bill.[37] Another scholar holds a similar view that the government's failure to bring much-needed socio-economic development in the region could provide the TTP an opportunity to regain influence.[38] The following section explains the rise of the TTP in recent years, especially after the Afghan Taliban gained control of Afghanistan followed by US forces' withdrawal from the country.

Resurgence of the TTP

The Operation Zarb-e-Azb launched in June 2014 has severely curtailed the TTP's operational capability by dismantling its financial capability and organizational infrastructure.[39] The US drone campaign has significantly contributed to this success through its campaign of decapitating the TTP leadership.[40] The overall strength of TTP was further degraded with schism and infighting within the group which started after the death of TTP leader Hakimullah Mehsud in 2013 in a drone attack. Confronted with serious challenges to the group's cohesion and losing territorial control, the TTP disintegrated into several factions and most of the leadership and members took refuge across the border in eastern Afghanistan.[41]

Despite serious losses to its operational capability and suffering from internecine conflict leading to breakaway factions, the TTP had managed to conduct periodic attacks against the Pakistani state. For example, during the 2018 national elections campaign in Pakistan, the TTP conducted a series of attacks against politicians.[42] Additionally, the TTP has targeted the national polio drive in Pakistan by attacking health workers and the escorting policemen. Terming the campaigns as a Western conspiracy, the TTP conducted several attacks in April 2019 against health workers in the Bannu and Buner districts in KPK, and in Quetta, Balochistan, that halted the government's national campaign.[43] In addition, two police officers escorting a vaccination team were targeted by TTP militants in December 2019 in Lower Dir District, KPK.[44]

In the last few years, the TTP has regained strength by reuniting with its breakaway factions. The TTP had weakened due to the better counterinsurgency operations, but under the leadership of Noor Wali Mehsud, the group not only revives its operational networks but also increases the number of terrorist attacks against the Pakistani state. The TTP's total attacks in FATA and KP increased to twenty-one and twenty-eight in 2019 and 2020, respectively, compared to a low of only twelve attacks in 2018.[45] Most of these attacks have targeted Pakistani security personnel, the police especially, although the number of fatalities has been generally low.[46] The TTP may once again establish itself as a major threat to the Pakistani state and its people if not checked by counterterrorism operations and other necessary measures such as curtailing their ability to recruit people.

The TTP's current leader Noor Wali Mehsud, who assumed as the head of group after the death of Fazal Ullah in a drone strike in June 2018, has reinvigorated the organization by taking several steps such as improving internal discipline and issuing guidelines to limit attacks against civilians.[47] The TTP's indiscriminate targeting in the past drew heavy criticism from the Pakistani public that provided peoples' support to the tough military operations against the organization ultimately contributing to the decline of the organization. The return of the leadership to the Mehsud tribe as Noor Wali Mehsud belongs to the Mehsud tribe, several militants belonging to Mehsud tribe returned to the group which has certainly increased its strength. Hassan Abbas notes, "the return of a Mehsud as the TTP leader ... persuaded many disgruntled Mehsud tribesmen ... to return to the TTP fold."[48] Most importantly, members of the Hakimullah Mehsud group led by Mukhlis Yar have rejoined TTP.[49] In addition, several other breakaway factions, including Jamaat-ul-Ahrar (JuA) and Hizb ul- Ahrar (HuA), have rejoined TTP in August 2020 and pledged allegiance to the current TTP leader.[50] Both JuA and HuA proved lethal in carrying out deadly attacks within Pakistan in recent years.[51] Hizbul Ahrar carried a suicide attack on a well-known Sufi shrine in Lahore in May 2019 and also targeted a mosque in Quetta in January 2020.[52]

Several other militants including the Punjabi Taliban groups such as Amjad Farouqi group, having strong links with al-Qaida, and the Usman Saifullah group, a breakaway faction of Lashkar-e-Jhangvi (LeJ), pledged allegiance to the TTP leadership.[53] These factions played a crucial role in the formation and expansion of TTP. About these merger, Amira observed, "cooperation between groups can often enhance groups' longevity and their ability to plan and execute deadly operations."[54] After the process of reunification and consolidation, involvement of TTP has increased in extortion, intimidation, and targeted attacks in Pakistan's border areas near Afghanistan.[55] Analyst Daud Khattak reports that the TTP has increased their activities in some districts of the FATA, in particular Waziristan and Bajaur, by getting involved "in resolving local disputes, forcing people to pay protection money, and targeting those believed to be their opponents."[56] These tactics were used by TTP when it became a powerful force more than a decade ago.

The consolidation of TTP through reorganization and the merger of different splinter groups has significantly increased the operational capability of the group. This led to a substantial increase in the terror attacks perpetrated by the TTP. According to a UN report issued in February 2021, "this increased the strength of TTP and resulted in a sharp increase in attacks in the region," with one member state reporting that "TTP was responsible for more than 100 cross-border attacks between July and October 2020." The report further revealed that "Member State assessments of TTP fighting strength range between 2,500 and 6,000."[57] Furthermore, according to the dataset maintained by Abdul Sayed and Tore Hamming, the TTP conducted 149 attacks throughout 2020. In the first six months from January 1 to July 5, 2020, TTP carried out 48 attacks, however, after the unification process stated, TTP conducted 101 attacks from July 6 until December 31, 2020.[58]

With the joining of two al-Qaida affiliates, JuA and HuA and an LeJ faction, TTP has been offered with an opportunity to inflict terror attacks beyond its traditional stronghold in the FATA tribal district such as Punjab and the provincial capitals of Baluchistan and Sindh such as Quetta and Karachi where these groups enjoyed strong presence previously. A suicide bombing attack in a luxury hotel in Quetta on April 21, 2021 which killed four people is a case in point. The actual target was China's ambassador to Pakistan who remained unharmed. *The Wall Street Journal* reported, "The Chinese ambassador, Nong Rong, was staying at the hotel … He was due to return there from a dinner meeting outside the hotel when the blast occurred, Pakistani officials said."[59] A scholar has aptly described the current TTP threat, "the TTP, even with its diminished capacity, will continue to pose a threat to the Pakistani state and its civilians as long as it propagates its extremist ideology and continues to recruit and conduct attacks within the country."[60]

The TTP has attempted to expand its support base to revive its fight against the Pakistani state. Apart from affirming its commitment to focus on military and government targets in its violent campaign, the TTP has attempted to woo ethnic groups such as Baluchi while highlighting their grievances and commending their struggle against the Pakistani state.[61] In propaganda video in 2019, TTP media wing recorded interviews with residents of FATA districts who blamed the Pakistan military for their suffering including extrajudicial killings and forced displacement.[62]

Likewise, TTP has endorsed PTM struggle against the state. These TTP moves can be interpreted in its quest to increase its support base among different groups engaged against the state.

After the withdrawal of the US forces from Afghanistan and the Taliban coming to power, the TTP renewed its pledge of allegiance to the Afghan Taliban and vowed to establish shariah in Pakistan.[63] The Taliban takeover of Kabul has generally bolstered local militants in Pakistan. The radical religions cleric, Molana Abdul Aziz, who is head of the infamous Red Mosque in Islamabad and previously supported the TTP, hoisted the Afghan

Taliban flags in Islamabad after the Taliban victory in Afghanistan. He then threatened the Pakistani authorities with reprisals if they tried to remove them. In addition, the Taliban have released Hundreds of TTP operatives, including the group's deputy leader, Maulvi Faqir Mohammad, from the jails after the Afghan forces captured them in 2013. Faqir vows to impose sharia in Pakistan.

With the Afghan Taliban into power in Afghanistan, the TTP has accelerated its violent campaign. It has perpetrated as many as seventy attacks against Pakistani security forces and civilians. Most of the attacks have been carried out against the security forces which indicated the revival of the insurgency. Brian Glyn Williams, Islamic History Professor at the University of Massachusetts, "The Afghan Taliban's stunning success in defeating the American superpower has emboldened the Pakistani Taliban... They now seem to believe they too can wage a successful Jihad against the Pakistani 'infidel' state and have returned to insurgency mode."[64] Alarmed over the growing number of attacks from the TTP, Pakistani officials have engaged the TTP in negotiation with the help of the Afghan Taliban. Seemingly, to initiate formal talks, the Pakistani government offered amnesty to the TTP militants in exchange for their pledge to renounce violence against the state, disarm their fighters and submit to the country's constitution as the supreme law. The TTP has reportedly rejected the offer of dialogue with the Pakistani state unless the state fully implements sharia in the country.[65] The Pakistani state attempted negotiations with the TTP would provide "the opportunity to [TTP] undermine the Pakistani constitutional order and promote its extremist narrative to gain publicity."[66]

Conclusion

Although, the FATA has been merged with KPK in 2018, but poverty is still rampant in the region with limited access to health care, education, and employment opportunities. There are also reports of widespread human rights abuses including arbitrary arrests, extrajudicial killing and frequent curfews imposing unnecessary restrictions on the movement of people. These factors combined intensified peoples' frustration. The public grievances are demonstrated with the growing popularity of the PTM which vociferously demands ending of abductions, extrajudicial killings, and military deployments in the tribal districts. However, the state has used repression to silence the PTM which could further aggravate the already existing grievances, providing an opportunity to the TTP to tap into them to increase its support base. The massive military operations have broken TTP's hold in the FATA but recently it has made some significant moves to revive itself using its sanctuary inside Afghanistan. The state should take concrete steps to counter TTP's narrative and ideology by countering violent extremism in the society. In addition, the Pakistani state should also undertake resolute efforts to improve governance in areas where the TTP once established strongholds and got recruits by exploiting local grievances. There is also a dire need to alleviate poverty by providing employment, education, and healthcare. In addition, instead of repressing sane voices, the state needs to provide venues to express legitimate grievances. Repression mostly tends to alienate the population which can force them to extend support to the violent groups. Bringing socioeconomic development and establishing rule of law in the tribal districts is indispensable to rule out the possibility of TTP's return to the region.

How would the Afghan Taliban's return to power in Kabul affect the regional security situation poses a serious question but devoid of any firm answers. However, it is pertinent to assess how the Afghan neighboring countries have reacted to the Taliban dramatic ascendence to power in Afghanistan and their strategic calculus in charting a course to deal with the new regime in due course of time. On 15 August, the Taliban took over Kabul, the country's capital, after a lapse of two decades, from when they ruled most of the country between 1996 to 2001. Since President Ashraf Ghani government's collapse, the Taliban have established their control throughout the country and focused on building a new government. During their previous rule, the Taliban could not get international diplomatic recognition because of their alleged connections with terrorists organizations such like Al Qaeda and their poor human rights record. Only three countries, Pakistan, Saudi Arabia and the United Arab Emirates extended their recognition. Currently the Taliban's international isolation is not that serious a problem as they continue to provide assurances to the neighboring countries to govern appropriately while gaining military strength against the international forces in Afghanistan. However, the regional countries have given a calculated response to protect their interests in the country. Pakistan's army chief Qamar Javed Bajwa in a speech on 20 August 2021 expressed his apprehensions in these words: "We expect the Taliban to live up to the promises made to the international community on women and human rights and that Afghan soil would not be used against any other country."[67] The Afghan Taliban have enjoyed close relations with the TTP militants along with sharing ideological and strategic ties. This would made difficult for the Taliban to abandon TTP or work against them. But going against Pakistan's interests would not serve the Taliban interests as they needed Pakistan's support to reach out to the international community for international diplomatic and economic support. For Pakistan, it would be unlikely to ditch the Taliban, but it would surely use its leverage to secure the strategic interests.

India has invariably approached its relations with Afghanistan in the context of its enduring rivalry with Pakistan. In response to Pakistan's support to the Afghan Taliban in the 1990s, India provided wholehearted support to the Northern Alliance which resisted the Taliban rule. In addition, India enjoyed cordial relations with the outgoing President Ashraf Ghani's government. It has poured nearly $3 billion in Afghanistan, since the ousting of the Taliban government in 2002, to help build Afghanistan's infrastructure and institutional capacity. However, the Taliban returning to Afghanistan in August 2021, India perceives an increasing threat to its security interests linked with Afghanistan. India's key concern is the terrorist threat emanating from Afghanistan as Pakistani militant groups such as Jaish-e-Muhammad and Lashkare-Tayyaba have close links with the Afghan Taliban and were involved in orchestrating attacks in Kashmir as well as in India. India alleged Lashkar-e-Tayyaba was responsible for the 2008 terror attacks in Mumbai that killed more than 160 people. India also blamed Jaish-e-Muhammad for the 2019 Pulwama suicide attack on a security convoy in Kashmir. Therefore, India is less likely to recognize the Taliban as Afghanistan's legitimate government, unless it gets assurances that Taliban would not allow the militant groups to use their territory to execute attacks against Indian interests.

Iran and the Taliban maintained inimical relations with each other before the US invaded Afghanistan in 2001. Their relationship experienced a low in 1998 when the Taliban brutally killed eleven Iranian diplomats in Mazar-i-Sharif. Even Tehran provided the US crucial support in overthrowing the Taliban regime after the 9/11 terrorists' attacks. Overseeing deteriorating security situation in Afghanistan under the US backed Afghan government and resurgence of the Afghan Taliban, Iran from the mid-2010s started supporting the Taliban by providing them financial and military support. The Taliban welcomed the Iranian support which in turn improved relations between the two. Now Tehran is delighted over Washington's defeat and vanishing of Western troops from its eastern border. With the Taliban assuming power in Kabul, Tehran sees them favorably. President Ebrahim Raisi marked the US departure from Afghanistan "an opportunity to restore life, security and lasting peace" in the country. Iran's government views the Taliban as "transformed" and "more moderate than before."

However, Iran is concerned with the continued instability and deteriorating economic situation in Afghanistan as it shares a 921km border with Afghanistan through which nearly a$2 billion of goods are traded annually which constitutes almost one third of Afghanistan's trade volume. Furthermore, Iran appears to support a more inclusive government in Afghanistan which is evident from its role in intra-Afghan mediation. However, Iran's future course of action towards the Taliban would largely be determined by the latter's ability to find a way for political and economic stability.

China's interests in Afghanistan are primarily characterized by the persistent insecurity in Afghanistan that could have serious repercussion for Chinese economic interests in Pakistan and Central Asia. Therefore, China has been struggling to improve stability in Afghanistan through continuous diplomatic and economic support by participating in US-Taliban peace process and regional dialogues. To protect its security interests, Beijing has long engaged all important Afghan political forces whether it was the ousted Afghan government or the incumbent regime, the Taliban. Following the Taliban's takeover, the Chinese foreign ministry issued friendly statements while pledging that China is "ready to continue to develop good neighborliness and friendly cooperation with Afghanistan."[68] Other Chinese official expressed hopes to engage the Taliban regime in a constructive relationship by encouraging the group to pursue "moderate and prudent domestic and foreign policies."

China has never viewed favorably US military forces' presence so close to its border. So, American withdrawal opens space for China to better serve its interests in Central Asia. Nevertheless, China has two pressing issues with the Taliban regime. First, China has urged the Taliban government to reach a political accommodation that requires sharing power with "all factions and ethnic groups" in Afghanistan. Secondly, it has demanded from the Taliban to cease its ties with the East Turkestan Islamic Movement (ETIM), an anti-China militant group having presence in Afghanistan. The Taliban have provided assurances regarding Chinese concerns over ETIM and made some advances to attain political accommodation, yet these moves are short of winning Beijing complete confidence.

Notes

1 International Crisis Group, *Shaping a New Peace in Pakistan's Tribal Areas* (ICG: Brussels, 2018), 10.
2 Earlier reforms were undertaken by Pakistan People's Party (PPP) governments that included extending the adult franchise to FATA in 1996–1997 and allowing political parties to operate in FATA. Reforms were proposed in the Frontier Crimes Regulations in 2011. International Crisis Group, *Pakistan: Countering Militancy in FATA* (ICG: Brussels, 2009); "Far-reaching FATA reforms unveiled," *Dawn*, August 14, 2011.
3 International Crisis Group, *Shaping a New Peace in Pakistan's Tribal Areas*, 10.
4 On 13 April 2018, the Senate had approved the National Assembly bill to extend the jurisdiction of the Supreme Court and Peshawar High Court to FATA. However, according to article 247, this jurisdiction could only be extended to those areas notified by the federal government. "Bill extending PHC, SC jurisdiction to Fata passed by National Assembly", *Dawn*, January 12, 2018; "Senate approves bill extending SC, PHC powers to Fata", *The News*, April 14, 2018.
5 "KP-Fata bill sails through Senate", *The News*, May 26, 2018; "KP assembly approves landmark bill merging Fata with province", *Dawn*, May 27, 2018.
6 "FATA's Historical Transition," *Dawn*, May 29, 2018.
7 Umar Mahmood Khan, Rana Hamza Ijaz, and Sevim Saadat, *Extending Constitutional Rights to Pakistan's Tribal Areas* (Washington DC: The United States Institute of Peace, April 2021), 6.
8 Amin Ahmed, "39pc of Pakistanis Live in Poverty; Fata, Balochistan Worst Hit," *Dawn*, June 21, 2016.
9 Cited in Khan, et al., *Extending Constitutional Rights to Pakistan's Tribal Areas*, 3.
10 Ben Farmer, "Pakistan's Tribal Areas Are Still Waiting for Justice as Army Tightens Grip," *New York Times*, June 11, 2019.
11 A FATA resident Khan Zaib interview with the author, Islamabad, Feb 12, 2019.
12 Saad Sayeed and Radha Shah, *Displacement, Repatriation and Rehabilitation: Stories of Dispossession from Pakistan's Frontier* (Berlin: Stiftung Wissenschaft und Politik, 2017), 18.

13 Imtiaz Ali, *Mainstreaming Pakistan's Federally Administrative Tribal Areas: Reform Initiatives and Roadblocks* (Washington DC: United States Institute of Peace, 2018); Wajeeha Malik and Shakeeb Asrar, "Post-Merger Inaction in FATA: Expectations Vs. Reality," *South Asian Voices*, July 10, 2019.

14 Ishtiaq Ahmed, *"Emergence of the Pashtun Tahafuz Movement," Daily Times*, April 14, 2018.

15 Ayesha Siddique, "New nationalist movement emerges from Pakistan's Pashtun protests," *Gandhara News Analysis*, April 11, 2018.

16 See Abubakar Siddiqui, "Leader's Arrest Galvanizes Pashtun Rights Movement in Pakistan," *Gandhara News*, January 30, 2020. Cited in Hassan Abbas, "Extremism and Terrorism Trends in Pakistan: Changing Dynamics and New Challenges," *CTC Sentinel* (2021): 45.

17 Mohsin Dawar, "Opinion: We are peacefully demanding change in Pakistan. The military says we're 'traitors,'" *The Washington Post*, February 14, 2020.

18 Rahim Nasar, "Why Female Pashtun Activists Matter for PTM," *Asia Times*, January 24, 2019.

19 Farooq Yousaf and Syed FurrukhZad, "Pashtun *Jirga* and prospects of peace and conflict resolution in Pakistan's 'tribal' frontier," *Third World Quarterly* 41, no. 7 (2020): 1211.

20 Yousaf and FurrukhZad, "Pashtun *Jirga* and prospects of peace," 1211–1212.

21 Nasar, "Why Female Pashtun Activists Matter."

22 Ibrahim Shinwari, "Pakhtun Tahaffuz Movement has no anti-state agenda," *Dawn*, April 2, 2018.

23 Siddique, "New nationalist movement emerges from Pakistan."

24 Madiha Afzal, "Why is Pakistan's military repressing a huge, nonviolent Pashtun protest movement?," Brookings Institute, February 7, 2020, accessed on April 9, 2020, https://www.brookings.edu/blog/order-from-chaos/2020/02/07/why-is-pakistans-military-repressing-a-huge-nonviolent-pashtun-protest-movement/.

25 Diaa Hadid and Abdul Sattar, *"Caught between the military and militants, Pakistan's Pashtuns fight for rights,"* April 7, 2018, accessed on May 16, 2019, Retrieved from https://www.npr.org/sections/parallels/2018/04/07/598045758/caught-between-the-military-and-militantspakistans-pashtuns-fight-for-rights.

26 Imtiaz Gul, "Handle PTM with care – Correction, not coercion," *Daily Times*, April 25, 2018.

27 Sanjay Kapoor, *"Pakistan's battered tribal regions set the stage for new prime minister,"* September 14, 2018, accessed on November 18, 2019, https://www.orfonline.org/wpcontent/uploads/2018/09/ORF_Special_Report_75_Pakistan-Imran-N.pdf.

28 "Gen Qamar questions motive behind 'engineered protest' over FATA," *The Express Tribune,* April 12, 2018.

29 Siddique, "New nationalist movement emerges from Pakistan."

30 "Radio Pak claims MNAs Dawar, Wazir 'fulfilling vested Indian agenda through Afghanistan,'" *Dawn,* March 10, 2020; Hasib Danish Alikozai, "Pakistani Activist Rejects Charges Foreign Spying Agencies Funding His Group," *Voice of America,* May 7, 2019.

31 Hassan Abbas, "Extremism and Terrorism Trends in Pakistan: Changing Dynamics and New Challenges," *CTC Sentinel*, February 2021, p. 45.

32 Farooq Yousaf, "Pakistan's 'Tribal' Pashtuns, Their 'Violent' Representation, and the Pashtun *Tahafuz* Movement," *Sage Open* (2019): 6–7.

33 Cited in Hassan Abbas, "Extremism and Terrorism Trends in Pakistan: Changing Dynamics and New Challenges." P. 45.

34 Umair Jamal, "Understanding the Realpolitik behind Pakistan's FATA-KP provincial merger," *The Diplomat*, May 30, 2018.

35 Harrison Akins, "Pakistan's 'Pashtun Spring' faces off against a colonial-era law," May 25, 2018. *LSE South Asia*, accessed on July 20, 2019. Retrieved from http:// eprints.lse.ac.uk/89990/.

36 See "Peshawar police arrest MNA Ali Wazir," *The News*, December 16, 2020. See also Mohsin Dawar, "Pashtuns' struggle for rights cannot be silenced through violence," *Al Jazeera*, June 20, 2020.

37 International Crisis Group, *Shaping a New Peace in Pakistan's Tribal Areas.*

38 Amira Jadoon, *The Evolution and Potential Resurgence of the Tehrik-i-Taliban Pakistan* (Washington DC: United States Institute of Peace, 2021), 21.

39 Abbas, "Extremism and Terrorism Trends in Pakistan," 45.

40 Hassan Abbas, "Are Drone Strikes Killing Terrorists or Creating Them?" *Atlantic*, March 31, 2013.

41 Daud Khattak, "Whither the Pakistani Taliban: An Assessment of Recent Trends," *New America Foundation* (2020).

42 Javed Aziz Khan, "14 Days Before Elections: ANP's Haroon Bilour Killed in Blast," *The News*, July 11, 2018; "Female Suicide Bomber Kills Eight in Northwest Pakistan," *Reuters*, July 21, 2019.

43 Shamil Shams, "Pakistan Suspends Polio Vaccine Drive after Health Worker Attacks," *Deutsche Welle*, April 27, 2019, accessed on February 20, 2020, www. dw.com/en/pakistan-suspends-polio-vaccine-drive-after-health-worker-attacks/a-48 510718.

44 "Taliban Gunmen Kill Two Pakistani Police Escorting Polio Team," *Radio Free Europe*, December 18, 2019, accessed on March 20, 2020,www.rferl.org/a/taliba n-gunmen-kill-two-pakistani-police-escorting-polio-team/30332121.html.

45 Jadoon, *The Evolution and Potential Resurgence of the Tehrik-i-Taliban Pakistan*, 12.

46 Ben Farmer and Ihsanullah Tipu Mehsud, "Pakistan Builds Border Fence, Limiting Militants and Families Alike," *New York Times*, March 15, 2020, accessed on June 17, 2020, www.nytimes.com/2020/03/15/world/asia/pakistan-afghanista n-border-fence.html.

47 Abdul Sayed and Tore Hamming, "The Revival of the Pakistani Taliban," *CTC Sentinel* (2021): 29.

48 Cited in Jadoon, *The Evolution and Potential Resurgence of the Tehrik-i-Taliban Pakistan*, 15.

49 Daud Khattak, "Whither the Pakistani Taliban: An Assessment of Recent Trends," *New America Foundation* (2020).

50 Daud Khattak, "Whither the Pakistani Taliban: An Assessment of Recent Trends."

51 Raleigh et al., "Introducing ACLED-Armed Conflict Location and Event Dataset," *Journal of Peace Research* 47, no. 5 (2010): 651–660.

52 "Pakistan Data Darbar: Bomber Kills Nine outside Sufi Shrine in Lahore," *BBC News*, May 8, 2019; and Abdul Satar, "At Least 14 Killed in Explosion at Pakistan Mosque," *Global News*, January 10, 2020.

53 United Nations Security Council, "Twenty-fifth report of the Analytical Support and Sanctions Monitoring Team submitted pursuant to resolution 2368 (2017) concerning ISIL (Da'esh), Al-Qaida and associated individuals and entities," January 20, 2020, accessed on June 17, 2020, https://digitallibrary.un.org/record/ 3848705?ln=en.

54 Jadoon, *The Evolution and Potential Resurgence of the Tehrik-i-Taliban Pakistan*, 14.

55 Niala Mohammad and Roshan Noorzai, "Experts: Tehreek-e-Taliban Pakistan Merger with Splinter Groups 'Bad News' for Pakistan," *Voice of America*, September 3, 2020.

56 Cited in Abbas, "Extremism and Terrorism Trends in Pakistan," 45.

57 United Nations Security Council, "Twenty-seventh report of the Analytical Support and Sanctions Monitoring Team, submitted pursuant to resolution 2368 (2017) concerning ISIL (Da'esh), Al-Qaida and associated individuals and entities," February 2, 2021, accessed on May 15, 2021, https://digitallibrary.un.org/record/3848705?ln=en.
58 Sayed and Hamming, "The Revival of the Pakistani Taliban," 35.
59 Saeed Shah, "Pakistan Investigates Whether Attack Targeted China's Ambassador," *Wall Street Journal*, April 22, 2021.
60 Jadoon, *The Evolution and Potential Resurgence of the Tehrik-i-Taliban Pakistan,* 21.
61 Sayed and Hamming, "The Revival of the Pakistani Taliban," 36.
62 Cited in Jadoon, *The Evolution and Potential Resurgence of the Tehrik-i-Taliban Pakistan,* 13.
63 Aqil Shah, Pakistan's "'Moderate Taliban' Strategy Won't Hold Up – For Anyone," Carnegie Endowment for international Peace, September 30, 2021, accessed on January 19, 2022 https://carnegieendowment.org/2021/09/30/pakistan-s-moderate-taliban-strategy-won-t-hold-up-for-anyone-pub-85462.
64 "Afghan Taliban's victory boosts Pakistani Radicals," *The Times of India,* October 18, 2021.
65 Abdul Basit, "Pakistan's Peace Talks with Tehreek-e-Taliban Pakistan: Ten Times a Failure?," *Terrorism Monitor* 19, no. 20 (2021).
66 Basit, "Pakistan's Peace Talks with Tehreek-e-Taliban Pakistan."
67 "COAS expects Taliban to live up to 'promises'," *Daily Times,* August 21, 2021.
68 Ministry of Foreign Affairs of the People's Republic of China, "Foreign Ministry Spokesperson Hua Chunying's Regular Press Conference on August 16, 2021," accessed on May 15, 2022. https://www.fmprc.gov.cn/mfa_eng/xwfw_665399/s2510_665401/2511_665403/t189.

Bibliography

Abbas, Hassan. "Are Drone Strikes Killing Terrorists or Creating Them?" *Atlantic*, March 31, 2013.
Abbas, Hassan. "Extremism and Terrorism Trends in Pakistan: Changing Dynamics and New Challenges." *CTC Sentinel* (2021): 44–49.
"Afghan Taliban's victory boosts Pakistani Radicals." *The Times of India*, October 18, 2021.
Afzal, Madiha. "Why is Pakistan's military repressing a huge, nonviolent Pashtun protest movement?" Brookings Institute, February 7, 2020. Accessed on April 9, 2020, https://www.brookings.edu/blog/order-from-chaos/2020/02/07/why-is-pakistans-military-repressing-a-huge-nonviolent-pashtun-protest-movement.
Ahmed, Amin. "39pc of Pakistanis Live in Poverty; Fata, Balochistan Worst Hit." *Dawn*, June 21, 2016.
Ahmed, Ishtiaq. "Emergence of the Pashtun Tahafuz Movement." *Daily Times*, April 14, 2018.
Akins, Harrison. "Pakistan's 'Pashtun Spring' faces off against a colonial-era law." LSE South Asia, May 25, 2018. Accessed on July 20, 2019, http://eprints.lse.ac.uk/89990.
Ali, Imtiaz. *Mainstreaming Pakistan's Federally Administrative Tribal Areas: Reform Initiatives and Roadblocks.* Washington DC: United States Institute of Peace, 2018.
Alikozai, Hasib Danish. "Pakistani Activist Rejects Charges Foreign Spying Agencies Funding His Group." *Voice of America*, May 7, 2019.

Basit, Abdul. "Pakistan's Peace Talks with Tehreek-e-Taliban Pakistan: Ten Times a Failure?." *Terrorism Monitor* 19, no. 20 (2021): 1–4.

"Bill extending PHC, SC jurisdiction to Fata passed by National Assembly." *Dawn*, January 12, 2018.

"COAS expects Taliban to live up to 'promises'." *Daily Times*, August 21, 2021.

Dawar, Mohsin. "Opinion: We are peacefully demanding change in Pakistan. The military says we're 'traitors'." *The Washington Post*, February 14, 2020.

Dawar, Mohsin. "Pashtuns' struggle for rights cannot be silenced through violence." *Al Jazeera*, June 20, 2020.

"Far-reaching FATA reforms unveiled." *Dawn*, August 14, 2011.

Farmer, Ben. "Pakistan's Tribal Areas Are Still Waiting for Justice as Army Tightens Grip." *New York Times*, June 11, 2019.

Farmer, Ben, and Ihsanullah Tipu Mehsud, "Pakistan Builds Border Fence, Limiting Militants and Families Alike." *New York Times*, March 15, 2020. Accessed on June 17, 2020, www.nytimes.com/2020/03/15/world/asia/pakistan-afghanistan-border-fence.html.

"FATA's Historical Transition." *Dawn*, May 29, 2018.

"Female Suicide Bomber Kills Eight in Northwest Pakistan." *Reuters*, July 21, 2019.

"Gen Qamar questions motive behind 'engineered protest' over FATA."*The Express Tribune*, April 12, 2018.

Gul, Imtiaz. "Handle PTM with care – Correction, not coercion." *Daily Times*, April 25, 2018.

Hadid, Diaa, and Abdul Sattar, "Caught between the military and militants, Pakistan's Pashtuns fight for rights." April 7, 2018. Accessed on May 16, 2019, www.npr.org/sections/parallels/2018/04/07/598045758/caught-between-the-military-and-militantspakistans-pashtuns-fight-for-rights.

International Crisis Group. *Pakistan: Countering Militancy in FATA*. Brussels: ICG, 2009.

International Crisis Group. *Shaping a New Peace in Pakistan's Tribal Areas*. Brussels: ICG, 2018.

Jadoon, Amira. *The Evolution and Potential Resurgence of the Tehrik-i-Taliban Pakistan*. Washington DC: United States Institute of Peace, 2021.

Jamal, Umair. "Understanding the Realpolitik behind Pakistan's FATA-KP provincial merger." *The Diplomat*, May 30, 2018.

Kapoor, Sanjay. "Pakistan's battered tribal regions set the stage for new prime minister." September 14, 2018. Accessed on November 18, 2019, www.orfonline.org/wp content/uploads/2018/09/ORF_Special_Report_75_Pakistan-Imran-N.pdf.

Khan, Javed Aziz. "14 Days Before Elections: ANP's Haroon Bilour Killed in Blast." *The News*, July 11, 2018.

Khan, Umar Mahmood, Rana Hamza Ijaz, and Sevim Saadat. *Extending Constitutional Rights to Pakistan's Tribal Areas*. Washington DC: The United States Institute of Peace, April 2021.

Khattak, Daud. "Whither the Pakistani Taliban: An Assessment of Recent Trends." New America Foundation, August 21, 2020.

"KP assembly approves landmark bill merging Fata with province." *Dawn*, May 27, 2018.

"KP-Fata bill sails through Senate." *The News*, May 26, 2018.

Malik, Wajeeha, and Shakeeb Asrar. "Post-Merger Inaction in FATA: Expectations Vs. Reality." *South Asian Voices*, July 10, 2019.

Ministry of Foreign Affairs of the People's Republic of China. "Foreign Ministry Spokesperson Hua Chunying's Regular Press Conference on August 16, 2021." August 16, 2021. Accessed on May 15, 2022, https://www.fmprc.gov.cn/mfa_eng/xwfw_665399/s2510_665401/2511_665403/t189.

Mohammad, Niala, and Roshan Noorzai. "Experts: Tehreek-e-Taliban Pakistan Merger with Splinter Groups 'Bad News' for Pakistan." *Voice of America*, September 3, 2020.

Nasar, Rahim. "Why Female Pashtun Activists Matter for PTM." *Asia Times*, January 24, 2019.

"Pakistan Data Darbar: Bomber Kills Nine outside Sufi Shrine in Lahore." *BBC News*, May 8, 2019.

"Peshawar police arrest MNA Ali Wazir." *The News*, December 16, 2020.

"Radio Pak claims MNAs Dawar, Wazir 'fulfilling vested Indian agenda through Afghanistan'." *Dawn*, March 10, 2020.

Raleigh, Clionadh, Andrew Linke, Håvard Hegre, and Joakim Karlsen. "Introducing ACLED-Armed Conflict Location and Event Dataset." *Journal of Peace Research* 47, no. 5 (2010): 651–660.

Satar, Abdul. "At Least 14 Killed in Explosion at Pakistan Mosque." *Global News*, January 10, 2020.

Sayed, Abdul, and Tore Hamming. "The Revival of the Pakistani Taliban." *CTC Sentinel* (2021): 28–36.

Sayeed, Saad, and Radha Shah, *Displacement, Repatriation and Rehabilitation: Stories of Dispossession from Pakistan's Frontier.* Berlin: Stiftung Wissenschaft und Politik, 2017.

"Senate approves bill extending SC, PHC powers to Fata." *The News*, April 14, 2018.

Shah, Aqil. "Pakistan's 'Moderate Taliban' Strategy Won't Hold Up – For Anyone." Carnegie Endowment for international Peace. September 30, 2021. Accessed on January 19, 2020, https://carnegieendowment.org/2021/09/30/pakistan-s-moderate-taliban-strategy-won-t-hold-up-for-anyone-pub-85462.

Shah, Saeed. "Pakistan Investigates Whether Attack Targeted China's Ambassador." *Wall Street Journal*, 2021.

Shams, Shamil. "Pakistan Suspends Polio Vaccine Drive after Health Worker Attacks." *Deutsche Welle*, April 27, 2019. Accessed on February 20, 2020, www.dw.com/en/pakistan-suspends-polio-vaccine-drive-after-health-worker-attacks/a-48510718.

Shinwari, Ibrahim. "Pakhtun Tahaffuz Movement has no anti-state agenda." *Dawn*, April 2, 2018.

Siddique, Ayesha. "New nationalist movement emerges from Pakistan's Pashtun protests." *Gandhara News Analysis*, April 11, 2018.

Siddiqui, Abubakar. "Leader's Arrest Galvanizes Pashtun Rights Movement in Pakistan." *Gandhara News*, January 30, 2020.

"Taliban Gunmen Kill Two Pakistani Police Escorting Polio Team." *Radio Free Europe*, December 18, 2019. Accessed on March 20, 2020, www.rferl.org/a/taliban-gunmen-kill-two-pakistani-police-escorting-polio-team/30332121.html.

United Nations Security Council. "Twenty-fifth report of the Analytical Support and Sanctions Monitoring Team submitted pursuant to resolution 2368 (2017) concerning ISIL (Da'esh), Al-Qaida and associated individuals and entities." January 20, 2020. Accessed on June 17, 2020, https://digitallibrary.un.org/record/3848705?ln=en.

United Nations Security Council. "Twenty-seventh report of the Analytical Support and Sanctions Monitoring Team submitted pursuant to resolution 2368 (2017) concerning ISIL (Da'esh), Al-Qaida and associated individuals and entities." February 2, 2021. Accessed on May 15, 2021, https://digitallibrary.un.org/record/3848705?ln=en.

Yousaf, Farooq. "Pakistan's 'Tribal' Pashtuns, Their 'Violent' Representation, and the Pashtun Tahafuz Movement." *Sage Open* (2019): 1–10.

Yousaf, Farooq, and Syed FurrukhZad. "Pashtun *Jirga* and prospects of peace and conflict resolution in Pakistan's 'tribal' frontier." *Third World Quarterly* 41, no. 7 (2020): 1200–1217.

Index

Printed in the United States
by Baker & Taylor Publisher Services